LEADERSHIP
MANAGEMENT™
CANADA INC.

Subjective Management Development
Phone: (604) 944-2181

BC Mainland

ID397548

BRIDGING THE LEADERSHIP GAP

BRIDGING THE
LEADERSHIP GAP

Paul J. Meyer

with Rex Houze and Randy Slechta

THE SUMMIT PUBLISHING GROUP
Arlington, Texas

THE SUMMIT PUBLISHING GROUP

One Arlington Centre, 1112 East Copeland Road, Fifth Floor

Arlington, Texas 76011

summit@dfw.net

www.summitbooks.com

Printed in the United States of America.

02   01   00   99   98   5   4   3   2   1

Library of Congress Cataloging-in-Publication Data

Bridging the leadership gap / Paul J. Meyer with Rex Houze and Randy Slechta.

    p. cm.

  ISBN 1-56530-279-6

  1. Leadership. I. Houze, Rex. II. Slechta, Randy. III. Title.

  HD57.7.M49   1998

  658.4'092—dc21

                          98–9018

                              CIP

Cover design by Dennis Davidson
Book design by Mark McGarry
Set in Galliard and Officina Sans

GEORGE BUSH
January 13, 1998

Mr. Paul J. Meyer
Post Office Box 7411
Waco, TX 76714-7411

Dear Paul,

Let me take this opportunity to once again express my high regard for you
and for what you stand for.

You have motivated so many people in a most constructive way, thus
helping create a new generation of leaders.

On a very personal basis, I will always be grateful for your loyal support.

I hope your new book, *Bridging the Leadership Gap*, will motivate its
many readers. You are so well qualified to write on leadership.

Warmest regards,

Here's a book that will enable you to become an empowered and empowering leader. Paul J. Meyer's powerful and proven techniques will guide you to tap and harness your God-given potential for effective leadership. By internalizing and practicing these strategies, you will achieve extraordinary success in every facet of your life and business.

—*Fr. Anthony A. D'Souza, S.J.*
Director, Xavier Institute of Management
Bombay, India

Bridging the Leadership Gap is a must-read work from three outstanding entrepreneurs. This book will help any leader serious about achieving results through people. The processes in this book are invaluable for anyone who wants to achieve important personal and business goals.

—*Ruth Matheson, President*
Leadership Skills, Inc.
Canada

Too many books focus on the trappings of leadership, not the essentials. These essentials can be learned and developed by following the advice of Paul Meyer. Those who possess leadership qualities can improve and augment those attributes by reading *Bridging the Leadership Gap*.

—*David Sibley, State Senator*
District 22, Texas

At the age of 25, Paul Meyer and SMI made a significant impact on my leadership development. This book will *Bridge the Leadership Gap* for you.

—*Dr. John C. Maxwell, author and founder*
INJOY, Inc.

Words cannot express the impact Paul Meyer has had on my life, both personally and professionally. If you want an honest, straight-forward approach to maximize your leadership potential, this book is the book for you.

—*Richard Hunter, President*
Creative Management Group, Inc.

This book is mandatory reading for anyone who is in a position of leadership, regardless of the level of responsibility. If your desire is to achieve maximum success and fulfillment from life, *Bridging the Leadership Gap* will help.

—Kenneth H. Cooper, M.D., founder
The Cooper Clinic

Whether you are already on a journey across the bridge toward highly effective leadership or still trying to locate the entrance ramp, you will find this book invaluable. It is a slight edge for experienced leaders and a textbook for anyone motivated by clear and complete directions. Paul, Rex, and Randy cut through the fog with ageless wisdom and set a clear vision of what leadership is like on the other side of the gap.

—George Geerdes, Chairman
Professional Development Associates, Inc.

Paul J. Meyer's principles in *Bridging the Leadership Gap* transcend time and cultures. Since founding my company nearly 50 years ago, I have enjoyed well-earned success. I am greatly indebted to Mr. Meyer for my business growth. I highly recommend all of Mr. Meyer's programs and this exciting new book.

—Toshio Sumino, Founder and Chairman
Autobacs Seven, Ltd.,
Japan

In a constantly changing world, every community and organization yearns for effective leadership. Many individuals possess leadership talent, but it often lies dormant. This powerful book awakens us to the opportunity we have to impact and transform the world while we pursue our own worthy objectives.

—Ian Fredericks, Marketing Director
Asian and African Divisions
Success Motivation International, Inc.

More than ever, people are looking for new leadership. But leadership lies inside all of us; we just need to cultivate it. Paul Meyer knows leadership from a hands-on perspective. His unique experience makes *Bridging the Leadership Gap* a must-read book.

—Jeff Olson, Chairman and CEO
The People's Network (TPN)

Paul J. Meyer is a genius at simplifying complex theory into clear, understandable, and practical action steps. *Bridging the Leadership Gap* provides a pathway to greater leadership, success, and fulfillment in life.

—*Paul R. Brown, President and CEO*
Leadership Dynamics, Inc.

In *Bridging the Leadership Gap,* Paul J. Meyer reveals the distilled essence of 50 years of meticulously chronicled leadership study and experience. He has lived it out. Here you read in clear, concise language the tried and proven steps for authentic leadership.

It's been said that the medium is the message. That's true in this case. Paul J. Meyer has demonstrated leadership in the establishment and overseeing more than 40 businesses in 60 nations.

I listened to a senior vice chairman of the Peoples Republic of China ply Meyer with questions. Meyer's modest but brilliant response must have impressed the vice chairman as much as it did me. The next day the Chinese newspapers carried the interview on front page in detail. I observed Japanese and American leaders hanging on Meyer's every word at a reception hosted by former U. S. Ambassador to Japan, Mike Mansfield.

Meyer leads more by example than by precept though he possesses a rare ability to communicate. Since 1960, I have read everything —countless volumes —he has written.

In a day of growing consensus thinking that stifles leadership, Paul J. Meyer lays out in clear and compelling terms the formula for *Bridging the Leadership Gap*.

—*John Edmund Haggai*
Haggai Institute for Advanced Leadership Training
Singapore

Contents

Foreword

By Drayton McLane

Leadership is a timeless river flowing endlessly toward the great vast tomorrow. Equally timeless is the need to shape and mold the river's channels. The unceasing effort to remanufacture leadership continues as men and women seek new ways to guide, manage, and motivate others.

This is as it should be—all of us should strive to improve our leadership mettle. The problem lies not with our desire to grow and become more than we already are, but rather in our tendency to readily accept, embrace, and apply flawed and simplistic solutions to vexing and complex problems.

In stark contrast, Paul J. Meyer and his coauthors have produced a new leadership and management creed—a methodology that is both practical and personal. They call this method the bridge across the leadership gap.

All successful organizations build upon three key strengths: an intimate knowledge of where the group intends to go and how it will get there, the ability of leaders and team members alike to focus on a productive contribution to themselves and others, and their common desire to do whatever is necessary to achieve a positive outcome. A leadership gap is created whenever one or more of these three elements is neglected or underdeveloped.

Meyer, Houze, and Slechta construct their leadership bridge as an avenue to bring out these qualities in your organization. The journey across their unique span is comprised of successive steps; leaders find themselves first challenging old ideas about what they are doing and why. Then, a new road map for achievement is created and internalized. Along the way, positive attitudes and self-motivation are created and fostered as well.

Unlike the panacea presented by the quick-fix gurus, this leadership bridge cannot be constructed overnight. Several months, even years, will be required to implement fully the grand strategy brought forth in this book. Fortunately, leaders and team members alike can apply themselves to the long task, secure in the knowledge that the end result will be as they themselves have designed it.

In the final analysis, that is the collective genius at the root of this work. Whether we realize it or not, all of us design our own outcomes. *Bridging the Leadership Gap* offers us a system for doing just that. It reaffirms our basic responsibility for success or failure and reestablishes us as the makers and molders of our own destiny.

Matters of business and personal development are far too important to be left to chance, and the quick-fixes that are legion in the marketplace have shown themselves to be little more than worthless. What you hold in your hands is a unique new strategy for dealing with the age-old problem of leading and motivating others. Paul J. Meyer's bridge is a leadership creed for the third millennium.

DRAYTON MCLANE
Chairman, *McLane Group*
Past Vice Chairman, *Wal-Mart*

Acknowledgements

*Deepest appreciation to Dr. Barbara Chesser,
Tonette Holle, Jim Moore, Amy Seeger,
Kelley Smith, and Vicki York.*

Introduction

Defining the Leadership Gap

What Is a Leadership Bridge?

The leadership gap is more than just a literary analogy; it actually exists. As a leader or manager, you may see evidence of the gap in many ways—in the growing rift between leaders and team members, in the increased dissatisfaction many team members and leaders feel in both their personal and work lives, and in your own search for a deeper meaning and purpose as you struggle to meet the daily challenges of moving your organization ahead.

Just as the leadership gap truly exists, the bridge that spans it is more than merely a literary creation. Every leader—at every level—has the potential to construct a bridge of personal and professional growth that will span the leadership gap. But until now, leaders attempting to construct such a bridge have typically met with frustration and disappointment; there were no blueprints to follow or signposts to guide.

This book is designed to fill that need. The bridge that spans the leadership gap is made up of five pillars. Each pillar supports a vital part of the span that bridges the gap between leaders and team members. Like any blueprint, the five steps are easily understood and easily followed. However, the strength of your leadership bridge relies on your own willingness to grow and improve; without that willingness, you will succeed in building only a shaky bridge. Without the desire to become more than you are, your efforts will not stand the test of time. With a strong desire to improve, however, you can build a lasting bridge that will span the gap between you and your team members.

The Foundation of Values

The leadership bridge is built upon a solid foundation of values—values that are critical to effective leadership and to the team you lead. Much has been written about values-centered leadership; most proponents of values-based management leave it to you to choose and apply the values that are important to you and your organization. To a certain extent, this is as it should be because no two leaders are alike, and no two organizations are exactly the same. On the other hand, certain values cannot be overlooked, for these core values represent the mortar and stone that serve as a foundation for the leadership bridge. Without them—just as without the willingness to grow and improve—the bridge you build will be shaky at best and vulnerable to disaster. With core values as a firm bedrock for the leadership bridge, it will stand the test of time.

For many years, *principled management* has taken a back seat to *profitable management*. If leaders wish to help themselves and our society grow and prosper, they must develop a compassion and genuine concern for colleagues and team members. No leader can afford to commit totally to the practice of making money. Leaders must pursue other important goals as well.

Highly effective leaders can mold and shape profitable organizations. But what goes around does indeed come around. Effective leaders can also empower and encourage their team members to develop and use more of their full potential for success. For too long, too few leaders have shown themselves willing to engage in this noble and heroic effort.

The leadership bridge is designed to span that gulf between team members and leaders. Indeed, the journey across the gap is, in a way, its own reward. The ultimate goal for any leader bridging the leadership gap is positive, goal-directed change. Without that kind of change, leaders and team members alike are doomed to continue to do what they've always done. The inevitable consequence of positive change is an organization that is more alive, more vibrant, and more uplifted.

Progress, Growth, and Change

Why change? Are not some organizations essentially sound in structure, attitude, and spirit? Are not some businesses doing well enough as they are? Certainly. The problem, however, is that the environment in which these organizations operate has a tendency to remain static. The only certain element in the entire leadership equation is unremitting change. Leaders, team members, and their organizations must change to meet it—or face being swept away by leaders, followers, and institutions who answer the clarion call of change and grow to meet the demands of the times.

The bridge across the leadership gap carries with it an implicit message to leaders who are afraid to change: Find someone who is unafraid and let that individual lead the team. In the final analysis, a frightened leader is a paralyzed leader. Such individuals allow inaction to suffice where action is demanded; they never really see the need for pro-active change. Highly effective leaders react to the changing times, values, and conditions in a pro-active way. The end result is that they and their organizations are always a step ahead.

As we move into the next millennium, those organizations which are a step behind are left to wither away. Whether the end is sharp and quick, or whether it is a slow, lingering demise, the outcome is still the same. Like it or not, every leader is faced with the awesome responsibility and mandate of change; the acceptance of change virtually guarantees a vibrant and thriving future.

The Leadership Bridge as Opportunity

This book begins—and ends—with a question…and a promise. As a leader, you are the only individual who can answer the question; no one else can answer for you. And, as a leader, you are the individual empowered to seize upon the promise of the leadership bridge. If you are brave enough and bold enough to change, you'll find that bridging the leadership gap offers astounding rewards. For you, and for every member of your organization, the leadership bridge is the pathway to dreams fulfilled. This is the promise inherent in the five pillars; it can become the reason for your striving and the constant driving of body, mind, and spirit.

But the question must come first—and it must be answered first. Remember, you alone can answer it. As a leader, have you the will and nerve enough to embark on this journey toward change? If you do, you can lay claim to your inheritance—a vast cornucopia filled with all that mortals desire. If you lack the desire, or if your own spirit is weak, flawed, or faulty, you will find that the paving stones for the leadership bridge always lie just beyond your reach. The opportunity to bridge the leadership gap knocks only once; it is knocking now. The decision belongs to you: Will you answer that call? If you turn away, you may come to find your leadership experience hollow, unsatisfying, and empty of deeper meaning. Like change, the opportunity to bridge the gap is fleeting. If you do not choose to accept this challenge now, it may never return. But if you choose to build the bridge, you will reach each new level you desire.

Whatever you vividly imagine, ardently desire, sincerely believe, and enthusiastically act upon . . . must inevitably come to pass!

Crossing the leadership bridge is a journey in and of itself...as much of a journey as your own life and career have been and probably more of a trip than you and your followers are bargaining for! Your destination—the inevitable result of bridging the leadership gap—is the fulfillment of your own leadership destiny. Your dreams are your inheritance; your vision is your birthright. Now is the time to begin claiming them for yourself and your colleagues.

1

Bridging the Leadership Gap

The Challenge of Effective Leadership

Highly Effective Leadership Defined

What separates ordinary leaders from those who are highly effective leaders? Certainly, most leaders consider themselves effective and efficient. But the truth is that very few leaders are using their full potential for highly effective leadership. Those few leaders have discovered an exciting and elusive combination of attitudes and actions that ignite the potential in themselves and their team members.

To be truly successful, these leaders build a bridge to positive and productive change. If they fail to accept the challenge of this task, the human potential bound up in themselves and those they attempt to lead remains dormant.

Efficient and effective leaders begin building the pillars of their leadership bridge on a solid bedrock of values...values built around service to their society, their organization, their people, and themselves. Each of the five pillars represents a key part of the span that is built upward from this important foundation—the five pillars serve as the platform for the bridge toward goal-directed success and change.

The first step—crystallized thinking—represents the initial pillar of the leadership bridge. Successful leaders crystallize their thinking to determine where they—and their organization—want to go. The second pillar of the leadership bridge requires the development of a written, balanced plan of action to achieve those personal and organizational end results. Leaders build a third essential pillar in the leadership bridge when they develop the desire, motivation, and passion necessary to carry those plans to fruition. The fourth pillar is built by the development of self-confidence—efficient and effective leaders move farther across the leadership bridge when they trust themselves and know that they possess the leadership skill and competence to carry out the plans they have made. Finally, truly successful leaders bridge the gap to productive change with their dogged determination to follow through regardless of the obstacles, circumstances, or criticism, or what others say, think, or do.

> *Highly effective leadership combines the five pillars: crystallized thinking, written plans, desire, confidence, and determination to achieve personal and organizational goals.*

Throughout history, our greatest leaders always knew where they were going next. They understood and appreciated the value of goal-directed activity. Everything they and their team members did was calculated to move themselves and their organizations closer to the achievement of significant personal and team objectives.

As an effective leader, you develop a positive self-image that gives you both the courage and the self-confidence that are necessary elements in a critical decision-making process. First, you and your team members must make a conscious choice of a specific course of action that will satisfy your needs. Second, as you determine to follow that path, keep in mind that each individual involved must be willing to accept a share of personal responsibility for the final outcome.

Additionally, bridge-building leadership demands the conscious assumption of control over your destiny...and the destiny of your organization. You control your own future and the future of your team through the development of personal and business goals that give greater depth and deeper meaning to every action.

Bridge-building leaders can write their own ticket to personal and business success. You can name your own price; success and fame, happiness and fortune are all the product of the decisions and choices you make. Anything you can dream of can be yours when you meet personal and organizational challenges with confidence and diligence. When you are building the pillars to bridge the leadership gap, you earn the right to the rewards enjoyed by effective leaders.

How do leaders demonstrate extraordinarily high levels of effectiveness? At every opportunity, they act with self-confidence, using their sense of commitment to their purpose or desire. Their aim is to fulfill and achieve a specific goal.

Typically, leaders do what they know to be right. Their value system—the foundation for the bridge of highly effective leadership—helps them put their team members first. Then, clearly defined benchmarks help effective leaders guide their followers—and themselves—toward predetermined success.

Although photographers always give a great deal of attention to making sure their pictures are in focus, the most effective photographers also give careful attention to choosing the appropriate subject. Even if a clearly focused picture results, focusing on the wrong object produces a less than desirable picture. You must not only "do things right," you must also "do the right thing." Selecting the subject of the photo and focusing clearly on it are important to determine the quality of the finished product. To develop a habit of focus in life and to direct energy toward desired goals, learn to say "no" to certain opportunities so you can say "yes" to others.

PAUL J. MEYER

Effective leaders do what is right and productive for themselves and their teams regardless of the obstacles that might appear and without regard to the criticism or opinions of others not directly involved in the effort to succeed. The willingness to persevere is a hallmark of every truly great leader.

All leaders lead...but most lead only to some extent. Few leaders have developed their leadership abilities to their fullest potential. Psychologists tell us that the average individual seldom uses more than 15 to 20 percent of his or her true potential for success. For accomplished leaders, this percentage is undoubtedly higher; but there remains in every leader a vast, untapped potential for personal success and organizational achievement.

As a result, many leaders exhibit inconsistent levels of leadership. Quite simply, few leaders have been adequately trained in the art of expanding their leadership. Along with the lack of instruction, many leaders clearly lack the experience required to heighten their own levels of effectiveness. This inexperience hinders their efforts to use more of their full potential for both leadership and personal success.

Why? Because inexperience tends to make many of us reluctant to act. We fear making mistakes because we do not know what we are doing or how we should do it. The inevitable result is the continued squandering of our potential. We fail to gain the fundamental and lasting leadership experience necessary to ensure the success of ourselves and our organization.

All too many managers and so-called leaders stopped learning soon after entering the work force. They have one or two years of experience; these are repeated thirty or forty times.

These leaders need to expand their experience. Years of service are not necessarily equivalent to quality of experience. Extraordinary experience and insight can be gathered in a relatively short amount of time when leaders push the edge of new markets, new ideas, and new technologies. Bridge-building leaders retain what works and constantly stretch forward into new territories of learning and experience.

You possess untapped potential for extraordinary leadership. To at least some degree, you have already begun to develop your potential and ability. What you have already learned, in part, you can master and perfect when you begin to build the five pillars that bridge the leadership gap.

Today's most effective leaders rely on the five pillars to guide them through difficult situations. They understand that their leadership skills are not created by situations themselves. Rather, they are able to demonstrate their effectiveness by their *response* to given circumstances, situations, and opportunities. Additionally, truly successful leaders understand a fundamental truth that ordinary leaders largely ignore: Nothing restricts the potential of highly effective leaders except the artificial limitations they place on their own minds.

To develop your potential for effective leadership, begin with the strengths and abilities you already possess. You are always stronger when you keep your successes and strengths in mind.

Vince Lombardi, who coached two teams to Superbowl championships, observed that when football games were over, it always seemed that errors got more attention than successes. The newspaper and television media would highlight, analyze, and discuss the mistakes. One day, Lombardi decided, "From now on, we are only going to replay our winning plays." And look at what happened to him and his teams—his theory worked!

PAUL J. MEYER

Using your abilities builds your own self-confidence and the confidence your team members have in your ability. You also deepen your belief that you can achieve even the most challenging goals and objectives. Becoming a highly effective leader requires that you begin leading yourself along the bridge to personal and organizational success. Truly great leaders apply courage and self-motivation to discover, realize, and utilize more of their God-given potential for leadership achievement.

Once you internalize the five pillars of the leadership bridge, you are ready to begin building. You already possess the tools and skills you need. The talents and abilities you already have will form the basis for building your leadership abilities. Your determination to bridge the leadership gap—to make better use of the ability you already possess—hinges on four key actions that you can begin taking now. These actions mark the start of your journey toward true leadership change.

1. Recognize and believe in your innate potential for effective leadership.
2. Develop a deeper understanding of yourself and the development of a strong self-image.

3. Learn to generate a consistent, unlimited supply of self-motivation.
4. Become a practitioner of goal setting.

These four key actions are essential to your success. Highly effective leaders possess a thorough grounding in these four areas.

Using Your Potential for Effective Leadership

Several times during the past few decades, we have talked with leaders who managed to convince themselves that they were already using a vast amount of their own potential for success. Contrast their response with that of a genius like Albert Einstein, who claimed that he was using only about 5 percent of his potential. Who do you believe is more likely correct in their assessment?

Compared with what your Creator intended for you to be, you are likely using only a small percentage of your potential for achievement. A striking parallel can be found in the abundant riches of the outside world. All around you, there are more opportunities for success and accomplishment than you could ever possibly pursue. All leaders—and all team members—are created to be strivers and seekers, to remain forever unsatisfied with things as they are. Highly effective leaders are not content merely to manage their activity and the efforts of those around them; they are driven to find a deeper purpose to their striving. When they are working toward challenging goals and lofty ideals, highly effective leaders are unsatisfied...but not dissatisfied. Poet Robert Browning understood this critical leadership distinction when he wrote, "Ah, but a man's reach should exceed his grasp, else what's a heaven for?"

As a leader, you already have some amount of desire to

achieve important goals and to find a deeper purpose and meaning in life. As a human being, you already possess the means and abilities required to reach your personal and organizational goals. You are equipped with a vital reserve equal to your needs. That reserve is your untapped potential for achievement.

Highly effective leaders discover that, as goals, objectives, and aims grow, they can reach into their own vital reserve to find new resources—new talents and abilities both within and without that will help to meet growing needs and challenges. Indeed, recognizing this untapped potential is the first crucial step toward meaningful leadership.

If you believe you are already using a large amount of your own potential for success, consider this: The scientists who study human behavior agree that few people ever use more than a small portion of their innate potential. In the final analysis, all of us have infinitely more talents and abilities than we ever use.

Remember that who you are—rather than what you have—is the measure of true wealth. The abundance of life is yours; you can choose to take it by embracing your innate potential. The choice is also yours, of course. You can walk away from the abundance around you by deciding simply to ignore your potential for success.

In fact, the greatest limitations highly effective leaders face are largely self-imposed. Before Roger Bannister ran the mile in less than four minutes, that feat was considered humanly impossible. Indeed, the four-minute mile had become a mythical barrier; athletes could not go beyond that boundary. But as soon as the world learned of Bannister's success, at least twenty other runners quickly achieved the same goal. Now, of course, the four-minute mile is commonplace.

Amelia Earhart was an aviation pioneer who decided to challenge mythical barriers in her own way. In 1928, she was a passenger on a transatlantic flight—the first woman ever to make the crossing. In 1932, she flew across the Atlantic Ocean by herself and became the first woman to achieve that feat as well. She was also the first woman to fly from Honolulu, Hawaii, to the California coast and the first woman to fly alone across the United States in both directions. Her Lockheed Electra disappeared into the Pacific in the summer of 1937, just as she was nearing the completion of a flight which would have made her the first woman to fly around the world. Amelia Earhart's pursuit of her dreams has inspired thousands to strive for challenging goals they might otherwise have been reluctant to attempt.

For leaders and followers alike, potential is virtually unlimited. Success, therefore, should be defined in terms that mandate the broadening of limits. Only by stretching your potential to reach new heights can you become truly successful.

Indeed, there is but one definition of success that is broad enough to include all of your aspirations but specific enough to produce belief in your potential to achieve any goal. What is this unique definition of success? *Success is the progressive realization of worthwhile, predetermined personal and organizational goals.*

Leaders are, by virtue of their profession, goal seekers. The greatest leaders are almost continuously unsatisfied; they possess a constructive discontent with the status quo. They find success only in the progressive realization of personal and organizational goals. For highly effective leaders, setting goals is not enough. They achieve those goals by working toward them on a constant, committed course to success. Their goals must be personally meaningful, and they must conform to and be compatible with their own deeply held inner values.

For goals to hold your attention, they must be predetermined. They must also be worthwhile—worthy of your best efforts. A leader's goals, in some measure, must call upon that reserve of inner strength that we call untapped potential.

Often, the death sentence for those who would become highly effective leaders is seeking success by comparing themselves to other leaders. Leaders who tend to evaluate their own personal and organizational success through comparison of themselves and their teams to other leaders and other organizations are bound to be disappointed. After all, the more people a leader knows, the less likely that individual is to feel successful. For the leader who succeeds only in comparison to others, life probably will be one big disappointment after another.

But let's examine the other side of the coin. You may be far more successful than your competitors, than your colleagues and team members, or even more successful than your parents and siblings. But you can still be a dismal failure; you fail if you fall far short of your potential and capacity for success and achievement.

Truly successful leaders know that the only valid comparison that they can make is between what they are to what they have the potential to become. Similarly, the only valid gauge of their organization's success is to compare what their team is to what the team has the potential to become. Ordinary leaders become highly effective leaders when they develop and use their untapped potential—and the untapped potential of their team members—and measure their success in terms of the progressive realization of worthwhile, predetermined goals.

As a leader, you already have the tools to begin developing and using more of your own potential for success. Additionally, you can help others begin to utilize more of their potential as well, once you have internalized and applied these strategies in your own life and career.

- *First, believe in your own potential for achievement.* Your dormant potential can be compared to a moss-covered rock sitting on a steep hillside. Once you give the rock a shove—once you put your potential into achievement-oriented action—it begins to roll and gain momentum. When you help other members of your team develop more of their own potential, the effect is compounded many times. Soon your single rock has become an avalanche crashing down a mountainside. Because of the unstoppable force of developing potential, you and your team members sweep aside virtually every obstacle that stands in your way. The momentum you have generated has true staying power.

- *Second, exercise an adequate amount of self-reliance.* You are the only one who can recognize, discover, and begin to use more of your innate potential for success. Highly effective leaders have learned to trust their ability through developing the characteristic of self-reliance. As a highly effective leader, you can rely only upon yourself. Just as you alone are ultimately responsible for developing your own potential, so your team members are ultimately responsible for awakening the sleeping giant that lies within them. You cannot do that for them; all you can do is point the way. All great leaders build relationships and loyalty that stand the test of time, but they also recognize that caring for people means giving them the freedom to make good decisions in their own self-interest. Ultimately, you as a leader rely solely upon yourself even while building and developing a team. You cannot be a "Lone Ranger" in the business world, but you must be able to stand alone when required.

- *Third, act with initiative.* The power of choice lies in the choosing. Highly effective leaders are extremely decisive; they refuse to wait for someone to tell them what they can or should do. They are pro-active. In addition to striving to breed self-reliance, highly effective leaders work to help their team members develop initiative as well. They understand that once team members believe in themselves, their leader, and their mission, they are impelled to act—they are transformed into self-starters who make free use of their own imagination and creativity as they work to solve challenging problems and develop new opportunities for success.

Self-Image and Your Leadership Potential

Once you have succeeded in recognizing and beginning to develop your own potential for more effective leadership, you face another challenge. Your next step involves the development of a strong, positive, and vibrant self-image. Understand that a positive self-image is not the same as conceit; it is nothing like an over-inflated ego. A sound self-image is, instead, genuine self-respect. It is a positive mental picture of yourself and your abilities that grows and blossoms out of the recognition that you have vast reserves of potential you have not yet used.

Sometimes even children can become stunning examples of leadership potential.

> My tennis partner's ten-year-old daughter normally played first base on her softball team. One afternoon, she was called on to pitch. After her warm-up, she threw three straight pitches that came nowhere near the strike zone. I watched her walk from the mound toward the dugout, thinking that she was embarrassed or that she would ask her coach to find someone else to pitch. Instead, she stopped at the edge of the first-base line and asked her coach, "What can I do to improve?"
>
> REX HOUZE

Until you develop a strong and positive self-image, you succeed only in greatly diminishing your chance to become a truly exemplary leader. Your self-image acts upon your aspirations like a gigantic, invisible barrier. It effectively sets the bar. Your self-image becomes a ceiling that you cannot rise above or progress beyond. Your self-image is like a line in the sand. "Beyond this line," your self-image tells you, "you cannot go."

Highly effective leaders have learned to overcome the negative or limiting aspects of their own self-image. Additionally, they have learned through personal experience how to help their team members overcome their self-imposed limitations and rise above their subconscious ceilings.

Leaders who harbor a negative self-image filter every decision they make through a network of subconscious fears and doubts. Worry, indecision, and negative thinking plague their management style. Leaders who unconsciously believe that they are not worthy of their position, who have a limited sense of self-worth, who believe that their talents and abilities are somehow limited will unconsciously refuse to achieve very much, either by themselves or through their team.

Strangely, these individuals can possess every other attribute of effective leadership and still be lacking in self-confidence. They tend to rate themselves so low—and to judge the world so harshly—that their low self-concept relegates them to the ranks of the stagnant leaders who venture little and gain even less.

While leaders cannot rise above their own self-image, they can raise their self-image. Leaders who believe "I can" are usually correct—they can and do perform even under the most adverse circumstances. Leaders who believe "I cannot," by contrast, are also usually quite correct. To be otherwise would be to violate a simple psychological law: People act like the individuals they believe themselves to be.

Does this mean that our greatest leaders are effective precisely because they believe themselves to be? Yes and no. Certainly, leaders cannot be effective managers of themselves and their teams without the belief in their ability to be effective and efficient leaders. On the other hand, the leader who tries to achieve maximum effectiveness through simple belief may find that efforts to alter subconscious attitudes and habits are frequently sabotaged by lack of skill, experience, and understanding.

Further, leaders who view themselves as failures will continue to fail no matter how hard they consciously try to succeed. True, these leaders may accidentally outstrip themselves from time to time, producing superlative results that fly in the face of their lack of belief in themselves and their teams. But after a brief flash of success, leaders who believe they are prone to failure prove themselves right once again.

An example of this phenomenon occurs almost every year on the professional golf tour. Around the world, there are several dozen professional golfers who earn a comfortable living in the sport, but they never manage to win a tournament. For the first two or three days of play in a major competition, you may see them lead by as many as five or six strokes. Sooner or later, though, they manage to adjust their game to their low self-image. Sometimes they'll tell a television sports commentator something like: "I've really been playing over my head," or "I just cannot believe how far ahead I am." Of course, the final result is quite predictable—they adjust their game to their self-image. They play poorly enough to lose the lead and any chance of winning the tournament. First place continues to elude these players simply because their self-image is a little too low.

RANDY SLECHTA

14

Why this dramatic cause-and-effect? Because a low self-image in turn produces negative attitudes—habits of thought—that hamper the development of personal success by forcing golfers and leaders alike to continually grapple with their own irrational internal fears, doubts, and worries. Leaders who cannot respect themselves cannot, in turn, respect others. Still worse, leaders who cannot respect those they lead cannot be surprised when members of their team fail to respect *them*.

For many leaders and team members, the central difficulty in maintaining a positive self-concept is rooted in early childhood teachings. Most of us have been taught that self-love is wrong. But most often, this admonition is rooted in another belief...the belief that self-love equates with selfishness. In fact, nothing is farther from the truth.

Human beings represent the Creator's finest work. The Scriptures tell us that "God saw everything that He had made, and, behold, it was very good." What God saw, of course, included human beings. Indeed, the Scriptures tell us to love our neighbors *as* ourselves...not *more* than ourselves, or *instead* of ourselves, but *as* ourselves. To become a highly effective leader, work to develop a healthy respect for yourself and your abilities; there is no excuse for doing anything less.

Outstanding leaders have always found that their power and ability spring directly from their own strong self-image. They have learned to appreciate their innate ability and potential, and they have developed a self-concept that is equal to the importance of the role they play in business and the other areas of life. Clearly, highly effective leaders have built themselves up from within. They do not fall into the common trap of using the external veneer of positive thinking to cover up for a faulty self-concept or a low self-image.

How do highly effective leaders work to improve their self-image? Over time, they are able to redirect their habits of thought and thus alter their attitudes about themselves. They learn to appreciate themselves and to respect and recognize their own importance. In a very real sense, highly effective leaders are the most elaborate human machines ever designed, and their potential for success and achievement is unlimited.

All human beings, regardless of status or stature, are unique elements in all creation. Nowhere on earth will you find two individuals who are exactly alike. There is, then, never a basis for comparing one individual with another. By making a deliberate effort to grow, develop, and unfold, highly effective leaders can make a contribution to their team members, to their organization, and to society that no one else can copy or emulate. By knowing, understanding, and appreciating their own personal strength and self-worth, great leaders build a strong wall of personal security around themselves and those they lead.

Leadership and Self-Motivation

A positive self-image is a vital prerequisite for the third key action in preparation for highly effective leadership. As you strive to improve your leadership skills, begin to develop a constant and consistent flow of self-motivation. Leaders cannot wait for someone else to point them in the right direction and administer a sharp shove to get them going. Leaders must motivate themselves.

What is motivation? It is an inner drive or need that incites or impels you to action. Indeed, the real definition of motivation can be found in the word itself: Motivation is a *motive* to *action*. Motive implies a reason, purpose, or goal; action is the "go," the "do," the act itself. When you set a goal and begin to work toward it, you are motivated. In other words: Motivation is a desire held in expectation with the belief that it will be realized.

The three key words in this definition—desire, expectation, and belief—comprise the three crucial elements in the development of motivation. To claim your own power of self-motivation, all you need do is develop these three elements. But how?

First, fan your desire into a white-hot flame. Just as a strong wind turns a spark into a raging forest fire, even the smallest fire of desire can be blown into huge, driving flames of purpose. Additionally, take time to clarify your own expectations. Truly great leaders are able to set goals and visualize their achievement. As an effective leader, you see yourself in possession of whatever you desire. And finally, in order to flame desire and clarify expectation, work to build belief in yourself and your ability to succeed.

Belief is essential in the development of motivation—both for yourself and your team members. Belief is generated by your own self-image and by the response your self-image evokes in your team members. Expectation, however, is even more basic. It is a product of the reserve potential that you and your team members already possess. And any desire—properly supported by both belief and expectation—can become a strong and motivating force. White-hot desire is the jet engine of achievement that propels you and your team members toward the goals you want to achieve.

Many ordinary leaders seem to think that self-motivation is a highly mystical attribute that is as mysterious as it is difficult to create. This is a myth; self-motivation is neither an unusual power nor a gift from above. In a very real sense, all motivation is self-motivation, and self-motivation is the calculated result of personal belief and genuine expectation. Carefully cultivated, self-motivation grows, blooms, and flowers in you and your team members. But it finds maximum expression when highly effective leaders prepare for it, attract it, and reach out to receive it.

I'm often reminded of one of our old maxims that dates back to the mid-1960s: Before you can hope to understand, motivate, and lead others, you first must be able to understand, motivate, and lead yourself. I think this is the first—and perhaps the hardest—battle that leaders must fight in their effort to become more effective.

REX HOUZE

The five pillars of the leadership bridge will help you build a clear understanding of the basic forces and universal drives that influence your own actions...both in a leadership role and in other aspects of your personal life.

As you internalize and begin to build these five pillars—crystallized thinking, developing written plans of action, creating desire, developing confidence, and exhibiting iron-willed determination—you will find that you are creating dreams and desires that you and your team members can hold in expectation with the belief, confidence, and conviction that they will be realized. This, then, is the essence of self-motivation.

The Catalyst of Goal Direction

Finally, every successful leader shares a common attribute: goal direction. This is the fourth and final step to take in preparation for assuming a new, heightened leadership role. Goal direction is the essential characteristic that allows highly effective leaders to focus all their energy and strength on the overriding challenges they've chosen for themselves and their organizations. Goal direction gathers the forces of your untapped potential, makes productive use of your positive self-image, and turns the ordinary flicker of self-motivation into a constant, white-hot heat.

Successful individuals through the centuries have confirmed

again and again that goal setting is the most powerful force ever developed for self-motivation. Nothing is more powerful than goal setting as a tool for developing and improving an individual's self-image; nothing breeds self-respect like the achievement of a worthwhile goal. Goal setting is the key to unlocking and beginning to utilize the vast storehouse of untapped potential that lies within all of us.

Most formal leadership roles begin and end with the working day. But truly effective leaders view their leadership role and responsibility as a constant companion. This is because successful leadership makes use of every facet of a leader's life. It involves every action, thought, or attitude leaders experience all day, every day. Here is the essence of highly effective leaders. Their leadership style is not something they *do*; it is a deep manifestation of who they really *are*. Whether at work, at home, in a social setting, or totally alone, truly great leaders strive to lead themselves and others through every area of life.

The practice of goal setting establishes a clear relationship between where leaders *are now* and where they are *going*. This sounds fairly basic...and it is. But the problem is that few leaders—few people in any walk of life for that matter—have a goals program. Why? The reason is largely because most people do not know where or how to begin such a program.

Most individuals have no clear idea of where they stand *now*, let alone a concept of where they want to *go*. This is the obvious manifestation of a deep need...the need for clearly defined priorities and values. And, for most individuals, grasping the basic concepts of goal setting is not enough. They clearly lack the experience to select and plan for the achievement of challenging goals. They require help and direction to put theory into practice.

Whether you realize it or not, your team members are crying out for that sort of direction. As you work to bridge the leadership gap with a clear and concise program of organizational and personal goals, you are empowered to provide that vital help. In giving of yourself and your experience, you empower yourself and your followers to share in more of life's abundance.

Leaders at every level know that while much has been given to them, much is also required of them. Internalizing and climbing the five steps toward highly effective leadership is a challenge, a method of answering the clarion call of leadership in a new and vibrant way. Highly effective leaders see this challenge as more than an opportunity. They know this is a chance to help themselves and their team members become more than they have ever been before.

The Rewards of Highly Effective Leadership

Your leadership skills represent your ability to obtain maximum success and fulfillment from life. Highly effective leaders know what they want to do and possess the confidence required to do it. They realize that the true essence of life is found more in the giving than in the getting. Along with a private world to conquer, each leader has a unique public contribution to make. As a leader, you may be more aware of the untapped potential that surrounds you. You are given a blank canvas, and all the colors of the rainbow are on your palette. You can create masterpieces that rival those of Rembrandt, Michelangelo, and DaVinci, or you can simply splash the canvas with the dull gray monotony of mediocrity.

The choice is yours. As a leader, you help conduct life's symphony. Ordinary leaders allow the tempo to drag and keep the volume low and unobtrusive. Highly effective leaders revel in all the variations of tone, tempo, and harmony that bring vibrant excitement to their lives and their organizations. Highly effective leadership is certainly within your reach and grasp, provided that you learn to use more of your innate potential for achievement.

All highly effective leaders feel within themselves an inspirational discontent or unrest...a certain dissatisfaction with the way things are. This inspirational unrest urges them to rise above themselves and their external circumstances. It inspires them to reach for higher, more worthwhile accomplishments.

If you intend to become a highly effective leader, strive to kindle within yourself that same constructive discontent with circumstances as they are; your responsibility is to make those circumstances better. As a highly effective leader, you will not be numbered among those who complain; instead, you *correct*. While some leaders deplore, you *do*. You do not lament, you *lead*. These changes come about because you have learned the principles and are practicing the habits that lead to the development of your innate potential for successful leadership.

While truly successful leadership is, to a certain extent, its own reward, you can expect other benefits as you develop and use more of your leadership talents and abilities:

- You will continue to enjoy the freedom of choosing your own pathway to success for yourself and your organization.

- You will feel the confidence that the life plan you've chosen to follow is correct for you and produces benefit for others.

- You will be able to eliminate the sense of confusion and frustration that you may have experienced when trying to please others by denying your own goals and aspirations.

- You will find never-ending challenge and excitement as you continue to strive toward developing the full potential that lies within you and each of your team members.

The greatest benefit of all is the personal satisfaction you will feel in knowing that you have contributed to the lives and careers of others. By helping others develop and use more of their potential for success and achievement, you become a willing mentor and coach. You help team members marshal their abilities as you guide and direct them into channels where they can find the greatest possible expression. Highly effective leaders hold this key benefit close to their hearts. Perhaps better than anyone else, they understand that in the process of becoming a true leader, one first has to become a true servant.

2

Values: Bedrock for the Leadership Bridge

Values and Leadership Identity

Highly effective leaders build a leadership bridge, along with their business and reputation, on a bedrock of three central values. These three values—stewardship, integrity, and a servant's heart—are critical to the emergence of an effective organization. These ideals may be thought of as the basic foundation of successful leadership. Without them, the leader and the organization eventually wither and die.

Without core values as the foundation, a leadership bridge is impossible to construct. A values-driven organization, however, builds for itself a lasting bridge. Through values-centered leadership, it distinguishes itself from its competitors in its ability to survive and thrive. A values-driven organization is more likely to know what it stands for and thus maintain momentum over time.

Outsiders observe these organizations, trying to uncover their competitive advantage, but they look in the wrong places.

It is not the obvious, visible elements like product lines, manufacturing processes, or even individual talented people that create the identity of the effective organization. It is the intangible values that make the difference. What too many observers do not realize is that without values, it is impossible to build a truly effective team...or to become a truly effective leader.

The first essential value of bridge-building leaders is *stewardship*. As a leader, you have been given responsibility—stewardship—over certain resources and assets. Stewardship can manifest itself on a number of levels, depending on the maturity of the leader. Stewardship, at an essential first level, is the wise investment and preservation of the assets of a company. The next level places emphasis on the invaluable, intangible assets of an organization—the collective talent of its people. These talents and abilities are recognized as the core—the human essence—of the company or organization. Truly excellent stewardship acknowledges human potential as the organization's most important asset. This kind of stewardship puts people first. Essentially, stewardship becomes selflessness.

Leaders cannot become truly effective—and are never really committed—until they are able to put the welfare of their team members ahead of themselves, their profit, and their own personal interests. Financial well-being is important to any business leader, but the quality that makes a leader truly great is seen in times of extreme financial stress. In a crunch, great leaders cover their obligations to their employees and suppliers before they reward themselves. This is true stewardship.

In organizations that fail, effective stewardship has been the Achilles' heel of management. Try as they might, the leaders of these organizations are simply unable to subordinate their own needs and desires to those of the members of their team. Short-term pressures easily crowd out the longer-term concern for developing people and their talents. The inevitable result: Team members feel unappreciated and unwanted and fail to deliver their maximum contribution to the organization.

Highly effective leaders invest time, money, and attention in the development, nurturing, and protection of their team members' immediate stability as well as their long-term potential for success. They recognize the importance of serving as efficient stewards on behalf of the organization and its members. They recognize this as the key to the longevity and profitability of the organization and on an even larger scale, the organization's impact on the economy and society through its continued offering of worthwhile products and services.

The second essential value of bridge-building leaders is *integrity*. All great leaders display personal integrity by being dedicated to the pursuit of significant goals in all areas of life—not just goals for the organization. Effective leaders lead well-balanced and well-rounded lives; their team members sense a house in order.

Effective leaders lead well-balanced and well-rounded lives; their team members sense a house in order.

Additionally, successful leaders offer their followers an opportunity to do as they do—not just as they say. Thus is integrity magnified and displayed. Gone forever are the days when leaders could closet themselves in an ivory castle, away from the prying eyes and close inspection of those they led or managed. Today, followers demand accountability and integrity in every facet of a leader's life—and instead of shirking that responsibility, the effective leader works to measure up to the demands of a role model.

Success and achievement are liberators—but they do not allow leaders to do whatever they wish. Like it or not, all aspiring leaders must display to their followers a willingness to pursue personal excellence on a daily basis. All leaders should take that responsibility seriously. Being a role model for members of a team is not only a mark of high calling, it also demands personal discipline and a constant awareness of those who admire, respect, and seek to emulate their leaders.

The third essential value of bridge-building leaders is a *servant's heart*. Successful people in all walks of life share a common goal: to serve others. Leaders who lack the heart of a servant may enjoy temporary success, but they soon become disillusioned. They lose their concept of what their work is all about. They lack credibility among team members and customers because they do not believe in what they are doing.

Highly effective leaders, on the other hand, succeed precisely because they are eager to serve others. They need no substitute value or ideal to gain success. Instead, their servant's heart is an attitude and an essential value that helps to form a rock-solid foundation for the leadership bridge…and for lasting success and continuing achievement.

Hard-headed, hard-nosed managers and leaders may believe values-based leadership to be a weak alternative to heavy-handed management strategies. Still others may believe that only weak leaders take the time to focus on potential, values, contribution, and contentment.

The problems we face today, however, compel us to chart another course. To begin to put society "back in order," today's leaders must sincerely desire to serve others. Developing a servant's heart is the only way to help others use more of their full potential. A better world cannot be manufactured. It must be created by values-oriented strivers and achievers who want to give something back to their team, their organization, and to society. Unless leaders and managers develop a servant's heart, contributing to building a better world is a virtual impossibility.

The Scriptures tell us plainly that "Whoever desires to become great among you, let him be your servant."

> I remember a story about a father who wanted to read his evening newspaper, but he kept being interrupted by his young son. The boy wanted to play. The father turned to a picture of the world printed in a newspaper ad. He removed the page and tore the picture into several pieces. He settled back to his paper, confident that this challenge would keep his little boy busy for a half-hour or so. Five minutes later, the boy was back with the puzzle completed. Amazed, his father asked him how he'd managed to put the pieces together so quickly. "Easy, Daddy," came the reply. "On the other side was a picture of a man. When I put the man back together, the world came together, too."
>
> PAUL J. MEYER

Values-Driven Change

"A leader," John Maxwell notes, "effects change." Every alert leader can create the change necessary to bring problems and opportunities to a manageable level. How? Successful leaders generate change by applying essential values to daily leadership strategies. They help other people change themselves and their attitudes. They make the world more successful by positively impacting the individual members of their organization.

Instead of focusing on themselves and their own success, effective leaders focus on the potential and development of others. People hold the key to our greatest success...and people *are* the key to solving our problems. By refocusing effort and attention on individuals, aspiring leaders prove beyond doubt that they deserve to wear the mantle of leadership. Realizing and recognizing that everyone has a life and a worth both in and beyond the workplace is a common attitude shared by highly effective leaders.

While it is true that most people spend more time working on the job than in any other single activity, work is not the be-all and end-all of anyone's life. There are other aspects to consider—and consider them we must. Leaders and managers must know and be genuinely concerned when a worker's child is sick, when their employees are troubled by financial difficulties, and when their followers are making special efforts to learn and improve themselves. Such are the hallmarks of personal integrity. They are also the hallmarks of a good servant, a good steward—and a caring, values-centered leader.

Unfortunately, that sort of concern is completely foreign for more than a few modern leaders. By keeping their heads buried in the sand of self-contentment, they foster nothing less than a negative, discontented attitude in the minds and hearts of their followers. Just like the leaders they serve, workers are entitled to a life of their own…they are not consigned to a drab and boring existence simply by virtue of their status. The sooner leaders recognize that positive attitudes and personal direction are lying dormant in every team member, the sooner our entire society begins to move up the ladder of success. To keep pace with change and to continue to impact their field of endeavor, effective leaders strive to help each team member develop his or her full potential for achievement.

The Challenge of Stewardship

Is Stewardship a Fad?

Leaders at every level are charged with a vital responsibility: They are the stewards of human potential. In the final analysis, they have the greatest opportunity to encourage the development of the potential of their team members. As caring and dedicated stewards, they daily demonstrate that they care as much about the members of their team as they do about their own status, their own profit, and their own business.

> The team is the business. Without the team, all that's left is an empty shell, devoid of human talent and potential. If leaders fail to effectively manage the potential of their team, they abdicate their role as stewards.

> RANDY SLECHTA

Randy's comment brings to mind a common question: Is stewardship another business management fad, like downsizing and outsourcing? Despite the publicity surrounding "fad"-based management techniques, they fail to deliver the promised results. "Total Quality Management" programs have typically produced little improvement. Organizational "flattening" tears apart complex internal communications and accountability structures. Downsizing can be similarly destructive. Since 1990, less than half of the firms that have downsized have seen long-term improvements in quality, productivity, or profitability. And outsourcing was the management rage until managers discovered it created more problems than it solved. More than a few companies have found outsourcing so incredibly difficult to manage that outside production has been brought back in-house.

Successful leaders believe stewardship is a vital, permanent part of their management effort. This is because they continue to see their team members as repositories of human potential. As stewards of potential, highly effective leaders feel an ongoing responsibility to help followers grow and develop in all aspects of their existence. If stewardship is a fad, the best leaders among us intend to make it a permanent one!

Stewardship and Partnerships

Every venture is a partnership—a partnership between the visionaries and those who work with them. Truly effective leaders create a partnership with their team members that goes far beyond the process of helping followers develop and improve themselves. Great leaders are able to mold a partnership that enables leaders and followers to dream great dreams, make noble plans, and daily pursue those plans together.

If you fail to adequately shepherd and develop the innate potential of your team members, you lose an incredible synergy—a combined energy that is an incredible gift, at once invaluable and irreplaceable. If you lose it or fail to marshal it effectively, you and your team will function at a level far below everyone's capability.

Stewardship of human potential is an ingrained and ongoing part of the job of every effective leader. Two critical elements—a keen sense of personal responsibility and informal, on-site communication between leader and team members—help effective leaders and followers alike become balanced, content, and productive. Instead of being a troublesome liability, team members contribute their potential to tip the scales of any business toward success and profitability.

Three Kinds of Partnerships

The best leaders become stewards of potential by forming partnerships with their team members at three distinct levels. First is the *attitude* level, in which the leader can effect a positive impact on the team member's habits of thought. Most popular leadership "fads" and styles miss this level completely, focusing instead on goal-directed activity partnerships or skill-building partnerships. This omission is a huge mistake. Unless team members' attitudes remain consistently positive and productive, efforts toward reaching goals and building skills will create little impact.

Effective leaders form attitude partnerships by demonstrating empathy and concern for team members. This is a new experience for some leaders; showing concern for employees is not ordinarily a part of textbook management technique. Most managers aren't leaders because they cannot demonstrate genuine concern. Showing team members real caring and concern is the first critical step toward attitude partnership.

Effective leaders merge curiosity, knowledge, and interest to foster *belief* partnerships. True to their foundation or bedrock of values, they hold a deep and abiding belief in every team member, belief in their ability to do their job well, and belief in their potential for even greater accomplishment.

It is impossible for any leader to truly believe in something about which he or she cares very little. On the other hand, it is quite difficult for leaders to lack belief in an individual when they are interested in their team members and know them well. And, when leaders truly know their team members, they are able to see their true capability and potential. With that potential in view, effective leaders develop their own belief in the value of the individual and in the potential of each individual's contribution to the organization.

Finally, effective stewardship depends upon a partnership based on mutual *acceptance*. Accepting team members as they are—with their human faults and failings—is essential to marshaling their potential and helping them achieve. Effective leaders demonstrate acceptance by involving team members in the accomplishment of the organization's objectives.

Followers feel hard-pressed to accept and emulate someone

who requires them to change first. Effective leaders are stewards first; they *want* to help others grow and improve. Leaders become true stewards of human potential by learning to accept people just as they are.

Unfortunately, many leaders and managers continue to focus only on developing the skills of their team members—to the exclusion of attitude, belief, and acceptance. They fail to understand that skill-building is truly effective only when the other partnership elements are firmly in place...and when team member values are shaped as a result.

Partnerships based on a bedrock of leadership values are a critical element of team member development. Values-driven partnerships allow effective leaders to imbue their team members with commitment to the organization and the overall effort. For the truly effective leader, the organization is a mirror that reflects the potential of each team member. It is the leader's responsibility to develop an adequate values-driven partnership with every team member. If you accept, internalize, and act upon this responsibility, you will find that most team members will respond to your stewardship efforts with greater dedication and higher productivity than ever before.

The Question of Integrity

Why Is Integrity Important?

True leaders do more than just lead others; they also focus on where they themselves are going. The most effective leaders know where their organization and their team members are going as well. Leaders are required to be individuals worthy enough to engender a loyalty and genuine respect among those they lead. Leaders at every level cannot expect followers to do better unless leaders themselves are willing to improve.

> I recently read a *Wall Street Journal* article pointing out what I had learned long ago in the "school of hard knocks." The article reported that a consulting firm asked several top executives to cite the primary factor in their success. Integrity was consistently given as one of the top five reasons for business and personal success.
>
> PAUL J. MEYER

The road of personal integrity leads to the bridge across the leadership gap. Effective leaders must become complete individuals first. A personal purpose and direction are the first critical steps. Then come balanced goals for six areas of life, and, finally, the three qualities that help ensure the achievement of those goals.

The search for personal integrity forces all of us to admit—up front— that we can do better than we've done.

But goals and plans for achievement are not reserved for the elite. These techniques are not intended for leadership alone. Focusing on the most important aspects of an individual's personal life is the key to effective stewardship and the servant's attitude of putting people first. Personal growth develops and inspires personal integrity in individuals at any level of achievement.

If we intend to help others do better, we are required to do better ourselves. Leaders who are truly determined to show others how to grow and improve must first be willing to grow and improve themselves.

The Measure of Integrity

Integrity is the quality of being unimpaired. For truly great leaders, integrity is something sacred; it is an attribute to be guarded and protected. By keeping their own motivation at a high ebb, and by maintaining personal goals and objectives in all facets of life, effective leaders are better able to safeguard the upright nature of their organization.

When leaders are motivated by their personal integrity, they are better able to help team members perceive possibilities, develop pathways to success, and follow through to ultimate achievement.

When effective leaders are motivated by their own integrity, they try to ensure that working conditions are structured to develop and maintain positive, productive attitudes and habits for team members.

When effective leaders are motivated by integrity, they readily accept the responsibility for motivating others to use more of their full potential for success. Additionally, they accept and internalize the responsibility for motivating themselves.

Successful leaders are motivated by their own integrity when their goals and objectives are born of the consistent application of their own ideals. Making a profit is certainly critical, but truly great leaders are also motivated by their innate care, concern, and compassion for their team members. They understand that it is their responsibility to help others strive to bring out the best in themselves.

As both a leader and role model, your integrity is measured by two compelling standards: whether your endeavor creates benefit, and an understanding of the long-term consequences. The question of benefit goes deeper than concerns for profit or opportunity; everyone connected to the endeavor must benefit, and no one should be forced to lose.

Long-term consequences should be carefully studied. They

may be hard to predict with certainty but are generally easy enough to grasp in the broader sense. Of course, none of us is gifted with highly accurate foresight; it's impossible to see with certainty the specific long-term consequences of any action we take. Still, we can virtually guarantee adverse long-term consequences from, say, clear-cutting the rain forests of South America. Many negative long-term consequences are readily visible; seeing them for what they are helps preserve personal and organizational integrity.

Your Quest for Integrity

In the final analysis, personal and professional integrity are easily measured by the leader's passion for achievement and by a personal definition of success. Leaders who believe that success can be achieved by harming or hurting the interests of others may find that their standard of integrity is somewhat lacking. On the other hand, leaders who believe that success results in a victory for all concerned probably have a high standard of integrity.

Truly effective leaders believe that managing team members is a critical responsibility...an element of success just as critical as customers and suppliers. By helping team members do more and become more, successful leaders help them share in the mission, vision, and purpose of the organization. Effective leaders can instill the drive to produce more, do more, and become more...but only when they possess enough integrity and unselfishness to be more concerned for team members than for themselves.

Unfortunately, many leaders see integrity as a limiting concept. They believe that integrity limits their freedom of action and their options in times of crisis or decision. Nothing could be farther from the truth. Integrity actually opens the door to a broader spectrum of options and opportunities because the practice of ethics, honesty, and fair treatment attracts to you better people, better skill, and greater goodwill.

Truly great leaders tend to stand alone—they can depend only upon themselves for internal guidance, principles, and values. Part of the challenge of standing alone is making sure that those principles and values are not compromised, that standards and ethics are not violated, and that the eagerness to achieve a vision is tempered by personal and organizational integrity.

Developing a Servant's Heart

Leaders as Servants of All

Highly effective leaders succeed in large measure because they consistently think of themselves as servants. They wish to serve other people because they love other people.

Values-directed leaders find that having a servant's heart produces unusual benefits…benefits that manifest themselves after years or decades of working with the same team, in the same business, striving within the same organization.

- Leaders who possess a servant's heart find that they are continually excited by what they do.

- Leaders who possess a servant's heart are always full of enthusiasm about the results their customers and team members achieve.

- Leaders who possess a servant's heart look forward to each new day with great anticipation.

- Leaders who possess a servant's heart are always striving to build an active organization.

- Leaders who possess a servant's heart are always surrounded by positive, productive team members.

Leaders who have a servant's heart are eager to help and serve others. In contrast, leaders who try to succeed without developing a servant's heart must find a way to substitute for this key value.

Without a servant's heart, a leader is forced to rely on one of several devices to compensate for a basic lack of values, stewardship, and integrity. You will seldom see an effective leader resort to razzle-dazzle. He or she is too busy getting things done to do something merely for effect. But leaders who are empty inside have no other choice. They must put forth a flashy exterior to persuade others that they, too, are successful and prosperous in what they are doing.

Developing a servant's heart—in every aspect of your life— is a life-changing experience.

Others rely on a sort of "Madison Avenue hype" as their substitute for a servant's heart. They work to promote themselves and their team members as something they aren't, with the end result that everyone—customers, team members, and the leader—is left confused and dazed as the search for a real, values-grounded identity continues.

Still other leaders compensate for their lack of a servant's heart by sheer manipulation. One human being twisting the goals and dreams of another just to achieve momentary success isn't a pretty thing! Neither are the influence-peddling and power-play techniques other leaders employ. All three are aimed at making the leader bigger, and all three manage to cast the team members into oblivion in the process.

Whatever strategy a leader adopts, efforts to succeed without developing a servant's heart work only for a short while. Then, the leader is forced to try another method...and another, and another. Eventually, the individual ends up morally and financially bankrupt, and the people who should have been served drift away to find other suppliers and other employers.

Developing a Servant's Heart

If you choose, you can develop a servant's heart of your own and begin moving toward the kind of life that this attitude makes possible. When you adopt this crucial leadership value, you change the way you relate to other people...at home, at work, socially, and spiritually.

Developing a servant's heart begins with developing the attitude of sincerity. Truly great leaders have learned—perhaps the hard way—that any show of pretense is easily penetrated by others. Interestingly, the resulting rejection is usually much more profound than if the individual had just honestly expressed his or her indifference!

Hundreds of years ago, unscrupulous merchants learned to use wax to cover cracks and imperfections in statues and pottery. The flawed pieces were sold as top quality only to be revealed as flawed when the wax wore off or melted away. The dishonesty of the merchant stood revealed along with the flaws...and the word *sincerity* was coined to describe something pure, genuine, and authentic...something "without wax."

All great leaders have beating within them genuine and authentic hearts...hearts "without wax." They strive to help others without a trace of hypocrisy and without adopting some kind of false front.

The Ancient Concept of Service

The Bible tells us that leaders must first be servants. The concept of a servant's heart has been recognized by generation after generation of great thinkers and business people. It has even prompted some of the best-known business maxims of our time:

- "The customer is always right!"

- "The customer is king!"

- "Our clients are our most valuable asset."

Someone once compared truly effective leadership to a game of tennis: The player who serves well seldom loses. J. C. Penney, who built one of the world's greatest retail store chains, recognized the necessity of a servant's heart when he said that "life's greatest pleasure and satisfaction is found in giving, and the greatest gift of all is that of one's self." But perhaps former President George Bush put it best when he said that "any definition of success must include service to others."

REX HOUZE

By striving to develop a servant's heart, effective leaders are paying homage to this ancient success truth. And they are also making the most important investment of their life...an investment that has the potential to pay huge dividends if it is carefully nurtured and grown.

When the best leaders demonstrate that they genuinely care about others, we observe their team members responding to that attitude. The end result: Team members want to contribute to the team, and customers continue to buy. Surveys show that nearly two-thirds of all business clients who stop doing business with one organization and start patronizing another do so because of indifference. Indifference toward others is counteracted swiftly and surely by the development of a servant's heart.

When highly effective leaders invest in their organization by developing the desire to serve their team members and customers, the inevitable dividend is even greater success. When leaders possess a servant's heart, customers and team members alike know that they are appreciated and cared for because of the leader's follow-up and appropriate personal attention. Business and team members just naturally go where they feel welcome...and they stay where they are appreciated!

Having developed a servant's heart, successful leaders tend to display these important characteristics:

- They genuinely care about other people.

- They have a strong desire to serve.

- They believe in what they are doing.

- They like what they are doing.

- They pay attention to details—small details and large details alike.

- They are continual students...always learning.

- They possess character, integrity, and honesty.

- They make working with them a pleasure.

- They treat each customer and team member as someone special.

- They do more than they are paid for doing.

Recognizing a Servant's Heart

You can easily recognize a servant's heart in people from all walks of life. A number of years ago, when I lived in Florida, I went to see one of the most outstanding medical specialists in the nation. I remember being quite impressed with his degrees, advanced training, and knowledge. But I was not impressed with his manner toward me: He treated me as a case or a number, not as a living, breathing, and hurting patient. I had little confidence in his knowledge or medical expertise because he apparently had little regard for me as a person. Contrast this with the experience my wife, Jane, had in Waco some months ago. She consulted a doctor and found in him a servant's heart. She described him as a truly caring individual, someone who was interested in her and her welfare. When she returned for a second visit, he called her by name and treated her with attentiveness. As a result, she trusts him completely.

PAUL J. MEYER

As an effective leader, and despite your best efforts, you will occasionally find a team member or customer who is dissatisfied. Rather than trying to argue or persuade, hold tight to the servant's heart—and remember to serve their needs above your own.

A servant's heart is also expressed through competence. No

matter how much an effective leader cares for other people, caring and concern are no substitute for competence! While all of us want a doctor who cares about us as a person, we also want him or her to be competent enough to make a correct diagnosis and prescribe the proper treatment.

When you have a servant's heart, you care…but you also can deliver the goods. Truly great leaders know that there is no excuse for living in a self-serving way—to look out first for one's self—because all of us are free to choose to live with a servant's heart. Viktor Frankl, the Viennese neurologist who survived harrowing years in a Nazi concentration camp during World War II, wrote in *Man's Search for Meaning*:

> The experience of life shows that man does have a choice of action. There are enough examples of a heroic nature which proved that apathy can be overcome, irritability and fear suppressed.

Frankl notes that human beings can preserve a vestige of mental freedom and independence even under the most terrible conditions of psychic and physical stress. Of his time in a death camp, he wrote:

> We who lived in concentration camps can remember those who walked into the huts to comfort others, giving away their last piece of bread…they offered sufficient proof that everything can be taken from a person but one thing, the last and greatest of human freedoms—to choose one's attitude in any given set of circumstances…to choose one's own way of life.

Your freedom of choice allows you to make a decision: You can choose to tie yourself to your limiting past or to move forward with a servant's heart into the bright sunlight of limitless potential. Successful leaders have made that conscious decision to change their attitudes and alter their behavior. The choice they make determines their destiny…and helps shape and mold the futures of those who work alongside them.

Choosing to Live with a Servant's Heart

When you choose to lead and live with a servant's heart, you receive benefits that are not available to those who live only for themselves. First, you make your own decisions based on your unique knowledge, your values, and your integrity. You do not wait to be acted upon by other people or outside circumstances.

Second, you can expect a more effective outcome from each decision and choice you make because living with a servant's heart sets up a predictable pattern of positive, worthwhile, and long-term results.

Third, your choices and decisions lead inexorably to the fulfillment of your own personal values. Frustration is the end product of working long hours just to impress someone or just to make money. But working long hours because you value the contributions of your team members and genuinely desire to help them achieve important goals will enrich you in more ways than just financially.

And fourth, there is another benefit that comes from choosing to live with a servant's heart: When your primary motive is serving others, you become more successful yourself!

When you choose to live with a servant's heart, you develop a better kind of relationship with your team members and those who help you succeed. First, you attract a different kind of people…people who hold your values and who desire the same types of opportunities you've created for yourself. These are not people who are interested only in a job and in the money it brings. Indeed, those kinds of people begin to feel rather uncomfortable around you. They are not likely to join your team. Stated simply, the decision to live with a servant's heart means you attract to you the best team members available.

When you attract the best team members possible, they reflect your attitudes and values because those attributes are what attracted them to you in the first place. They become a genuine part of your team effort. They become as committed to service as you are. You can depend upon them to be positive, enthusiastic, caring, and committed to helping the organization succeed and thrive.

Having a servant's heart allows you to support and develop the self-esteem of your team members. You become an active contributor to their success. They repay you with loyalty, commitment, and increased productivity.

And, finally, a servant's heart gives you an almost unfair advantage in a competitive marketplace. Somehow, in some way, you and your team are empowered to make the right things happen at precisely the right time.

Values as Bedrock

Foundation of the Leadership Bridge . . .

By developing the values of stewardship, integrity, and a servant's heart, leaders lay the foundation for a bridge that crosses the leadership gap. When highly effective leaders put these three values in the forefront of their mind, they achieve more of their own goals than they would by putting their personal concerns and needs ahead of values and principles.

- Leaders who desire fame find it by helping to promote and develop others.

- Leaders who want to earn money find it when they sincerely serve others.

- Leaders who want friends find them when they have the integrity necessary to be a friend to others.

- Leaders who want love find it by loving others.

- Leaders who desire a sense of achievement are stewards of human potential, dedicated to helping others succeed.

. . . to Lasting Success

When aspiring leaders strive to become stewards of human potential, they begin to achieve their own personal goals while making a unique contribution to the lives of their team members.

When highly effective leaders are possessed of personal and professional integrity, their efforts bring about solid and stable organizations that prosper, grow, and stand the test of time.

And when extraordinary leaders develop a servant's heart, they find a unique synergy that springs from their sincerity. The more they give, the more they have to give. The more they serve, the more they are able to serve.

Wilhelmina became queen of the Netherlands when she was only ten years old. Until she came of age in 1898, her mother governed as queen regent. At her first appearance as queen, Wilhelmina stood on the balcony of her palace in Amsterdam and stared with wonder at her cheering subjects. "Mama," she asked, "Do all these people belong to me?" "No, my child," replied the queen regent. "It is you who belong to all these people."

RANDY SLECHTA

Can someone still construct the five pillars of the leadership bridge without bothering to build the foundation on stewardship, integrity, and a servant's heart? Of course...but failing to build a bedrock of appropriate values robs the five pillars of their ability to withstand time, pressure, and the winds of change. Some years ago, a town faced with replacing the municipal water system found that the reason behind a diminishing water supply was that the main valves had never been fully turned on. Similarly, you can construct the five pillars of the leadership bridge without basing your effort on a bedrock of values. But without stewardship, integrity, and a servant's heart, you will never be able to fully access the power inherent in each pillar.

Making Your Decision

The choice is yours. Truly successful leaders achieve the ranks of leadership and management superstars because they have built a foundation for their success...a foundation of values appropriate to the achievement of the goals they desire.

Leaders who fall short of their dreams, expectations, and potential frequently find that their underlying foundation is faulty, flawed, or underdeveloped. Focusing solely on one's self-interest, giving no thought to principles or values, succeeds only in shortcutting the five pillars of the leadership bridge. The inevitable result, of course, is a shortcutting of any success that just happens to follow.

In the final analysis, only one person can decide whether to adopt the attitudes and values conducive to highly effective leadership or whether to try to become successful without that critical foundation. That person, of course, is you. As you begin to construct the five pillars of the leadership bridge, you must decide whether to let the sands of wavering values and attitudes forever shift beneath your feet...or whether to build a foundation that will stand the test of your success.

3

Building the Leadership Bridge

The Driving Force of Vision

Some decades ago, a fifteen-year-old boy named John Goddard made a list of all the things he wanted to do in his lifetime. When he had finished the list, he had 127 items that became the blueprint for his life. Some of his earlier accomplishments were relatively easy: He became an Eagle Scout, learned to type fifty words a minute, and studied Jujitsu.

Some other goals Goddard set were a little more unusual: milk a rattlesnake, read the entire encyclopedia, and enjoy the thrill of a parachute jump. Then there were goals that to the average person might seem utterly impossible: climb Mt. Everest, visit every country in the world, go to the moon.

Now the amazing part of the story: By the age of forty-seven, John Goddard had accomplished 103 items on his original list of 127. Goddard was motivated to identify important dreams and to begin working on them by hearing older people say, "If only I had done this or that when I was younger." He realized that too many people miss all the fun, excitement, and thrills of life because they do not plan ahead. Making the list—creating the vision—was the beginning of Goddard's success.

Today, at age seventy-five, Goddard's list numbers more than four hundred. He says he's too busy to keep count of how many of those items he's achieved…but you can bet that the percentage is quite high! Goddard's vision continues to lead him toward new mountaintops…and continues to ensure his lasting success.

Creating Your Bridge

Your efforts to create a bridge across the leadership gap should begin with the same sort of mission that motivated John Goddard to succeed. Certainly that vision is not the same for every leader. For some, it may be achievement of a high political office; for others it might be the accumulation of wealth, the creation of a large business organization, or a prestigious social standing. Others may be driven by the need to be of service to others.

While success does mean different things to different leaders, we've already developed a definition that fits any vision for effective leadership. Remember the definition?

Success is the progressive realization of worthwhile, predetermined personal and organizational goals.

Great leadership is not something that is created by accident; you can't buy it, inherit it, or create it with no effort or forethought. Superlative leadership depends on following a lifelong process of goal setting and achievement. Highly effective leaders work to instill the mechanics of that process in the minds and hearts of their team members. Such a process operates through "progressive realization." Leadership success depends upon team and leader alike seeking predetermined goals.

This kind of success does not materialize through luck or by accident. Although many worthwhile achievements come as side effects of some other purpose, they are, nevertheless, a direct consequence of the pursuit of predetermined goals. It is true that we cannot always foresee the full ultimate effect of reaching a specific goal, but the important point to recognize is the fact that achievement comes as a direct consequence of moving yourself and your organization toward predetermined goals.

An incident in the life of inventor Thomas A. Edison illustrates the relationship between predetermined goals and unanticipated accomplishments. While Edison was working on a complex problem related to telephone communication, he had an idea for producing a machine that would record and play back the human voice. He hastily drew a sketch, handed it to one of his laboratory assistants, and said, "Build one of these." That machine was the first phonograph, the forerunner of all the sophisticated devices we enjoy today for recording and playing back the human voice and music of all kinds. Edison's invention grew out of its relationship to a totally different problem he had set out to solve. Had he not been working toward another predetermined goal, this invention would not have been visualized.

Whether for yourself or for your organization, the goals you set must also be worthwhile. Many people today are spending their time much like Don Quixote, the windmill-tilter who chose to pursue numerous idealistic, impractical goals. Too many leaders lose any chance for effectiveness because they spend their time and effort chasing rainbows and making much ado about nothing. They are merely busy being busy; they never achieve anything worthwhile either for themselves or for their organization because their objectives are unworthy of their efforts. As a result, they themselves can never feel truly successful or highly effective.

The final requirement for a vision capable of reaching the pinnacle of highly effective leadership is the development of goals that are personally meaningful to you and those you lead. They must fit your own values, standards, and desires…and those of your team members as well. Goals must meet both personal and organizational needs. Unless this requirement is met, you will find it impossible to keep yourself and your team interested and committed to reaching specific goals.

Building Your Five Pillars

A History

When I was nineteen years old, I wrote down for myself the five steps that I felt were necessary for achieving a high level of leadership success and effectiveness. Actually, I wrote the first four steps, then added the fifth step later when I found that determination and personal responsibility were the hallmarks of leadership success. I determined to use the five steps as a guide, and they helped me build an agency that led the insurance industry while I was still in my twenties. In the decades since, I've used the same five steps to build and lead more than forty companies. That's why I call them the Five Pillars of the Leadership Bridge. The five steps of this plan will work for you as successfully as they have worked for me over the years.

PAUL J. MEYER

Pillar One: Crystallizing Your Thinking

The first pillar in the support structure for the leadership bridge involves crystallizing your thinking so that you know where you stand now and where you want yourself and your organization to go. Remember: You and your team members will never reach goals by stumbling upon them in the dark. You need a well-lighted path, a well-conceived plan or road map. Developing a mission, vision, and purpose for yourself and your team is critically important. Just as you and your family would not begin a vacation trip without a clear destination in mind, you must begin the journey toward highly effective leadership armed with a clear idea of where you are going and why.

If you are not now making the progress you'd like to make and are capable of making, it is simply because your goals are not clearly defined.

The process of creating your own statements of vision, mission, and purpose actually help you to examine all six areas of your own life: financial and career, physical and health, family and home, mental and educational, spiritual and ethical, and social and cultural.

As you and your team members work to develop vision, mission, and purpose statements for your organization, those you lead will encounter the same need for the same sort of self-evaluation. Perhaps for the first time, your followers will develop a clear understanding of why they're doing what they're doing...of the purpose behind their work. Additionally, the development of a team mission, vision, and purpose helps members of your organization tie their personal success to the overall success of the entire organization.

You and your team members may be able to generate an impressive list of organizational objectives. Quite likely, you will observe that some of the items on the list of objectives are in conflict with other items on the list.

It becomes necessary, then, to assign a priority to each organizational goal or objective. Establish priorities according to a clear-cut system of organizational values—the truths you and your team hold dear and sacred. These values are revealed and created as your organization evaluates where it is and where it wants to go.

No one else can establish priorities for you and your team. The entire organization must accept the responsibility for setting priorities according to the team members' own unique sense of values and experiences.

Pillar Two: Developing a Written Plan of Action

The second pillar of the leadership bridge involves the development of a written plan for achieving your organization's goal—and your personal goals as well—along with deadlines for their attainment. It is extremely important that this plan be a written one. You and your team members are continuously bombarded from all sides by demands on your time and attention. Because all of us live in such a hurry, what seems crystal clear today may easily become vague or forgotten in the urgency of tomorrow's affairs. Unless you write down your personal and organizational goals, they are often lost in the shuffle and excitement of new problems, new challenges, and new decisions. Written goals keep you and your team members on course, on the track to progress, and help to eliminate outside distractions and interruptions.

Additionally, written goals serve as a point of reference and a reminder of the organization's objective. A written plan for achieving your own personal goals also contributes to your effectiveness by conserving time and energy. Because you and your team members know at all times where you want to go, it becomes easier to determine what to do next. A written plan also helps you and your followers spot conflicts between various goals and values. As a team, you can then assign appropriate priorities before those conflicts produce personal frustration or sabotage your organization's goal setting plan.

Setting a deadline for achieving your goal is also extremely important. When you and your team members set a deadline, you act on the deadline because the deadline acts on all of you. A deadline alerts our body chemistry to react to the timetables we have set. As a consequence, we think, act, and react with urgency and with appropriate energy. Just as our muscles prepare in one way when we stoop over to pick up the morning paper and react in an entirely different manner when we prepare to lift a one-hundred-pound barbell, so our minds prepare our bodies and our attitudes for responding appropriately to the deadlines we have set for ourselves and our organization.

Deadlines create a challenge; you and your team members will find yourselves responding to that challenge. In competitive sports that include deadlines—such as basketball, soccer, or football—the tension mounts as time runs out. The most exciting plays are often in the last few minutes, especially if the game is a close one, because people respond in dramatic fashion to the challenge of deadlines.

Deadlines also help you and your team members maintain a positive mental attitude. They focus attention and concentration on the key objectives at hand. They enable you and your team to eliminate distractions and to think clearly and creatively. You may have noticed that busy people are more positive than individuals who are idle. For you and your team members, physical and mental health are stimulated by the creative activity necessary to reach the deadlines you have set in the plans you've made.

Deadlines must, of course, be handled with mature understanding. You—not the deadline—are the master. Sometimes through miscalculation or unforeseen circumstances, you and your organization will not reach a particular goal by the deadline you have set. Because you and your followers have set your own deadlines, you can change them. You can adjust, reset your sights in view of altered circumstances, and change a deadline without abandoning the goal.

> *The mark of self-motivated individuals is their ability to distinguish between a setback and a defeat.*

The next element in developing a written plan for achieving personal and organizational goals lies in defining the obstacles and roadblocks that might stand between you and your team and the achievement of the objective. This part of the process is not merely making up excuses for something your organization has not already done. It is taking a realistic look at what you and your followers can expect as you work toward achieving a particular goal.

Obstacles and roadblocks may be the result of either *individual* or *environmental* conflicts. You may find that individuals experience achievement barriers that arise from a need for further growth on their part—more education, more experience, or the need to acquire a new skill. They also may include the need to develop personality characteristics that increase the likelihood of reaching a particular goal. Such personality characteristics might include learning better communication skills, avoiding procrastination, or becoming more decisive.

Other barriers involve the environment in which you live and work. In such cases, you may need to change the surrounding environment, move to another one, or alter the goal to fit into the existing environment. But don't be too quick to blame environmental conditions for your team's failure to reach your goal. Those who habitually blame "conditions" for any difficulty are often leaders who shift with the wind and tide. Regardless of their efforts to change their circumstances, these leaders and their teams never adjust to any environmental conditions.

Of course, there are times when *environmental obstacles* really do exist. It is difficult to establish a thriving petroleum refinery in a country where there is no petroleum. You are also unlikely to succeed if you begin a tropical fruit operation near the Arctic Circle. But most often, if you and your team members are honest with yourselves, you will find that obstacles are really manifestations of a deeper challenge: the opportunity to develop and use more of your own innate potential for achievement.

The third type of roadblock or obstacle you and your team may face is one of *conflict*. Many highly desirable goals, when written out and compared to other personal and organizational goals, conflict either with an established value system or with the time requirements of other, more important goals. If you and your associates have done a thorough job of organizational analysis and have established clear priorities, it is fairly easy to recognize conflict and to assign various goals involved to a proper priority.

Sometimes a conflict between goals is merely a matter of timing. While two goals may be equally important, one may be urgent while the other could easily be postponed until some later time. For example, you may have a goal to develop a new product line to generate additional sales. You may also have a goal to increase sales of existing product line. The two goals may actually complement each other, or you may realize that it is impossible to do both at the same time. You may solve the conflict by moving your new product introduction to a later time, allowing you the opportunity to strengthen sales of the current products. Here, as in so many instances, a written plan helps you and your team members anticipate such conflicts and plan how to deal with them before they become a source of frustration.

Identifying the obstacles and roadblocks that block the speedy achievement of organizational goals is, in many cases, the hardest part of finding a path to their accomplishment. When you and your team members have a written summary of the potential obstacles that stand between you and your goals, the next step is to plan a solution for overcoming each of them. Consider each obstacle or roadblock separately and devise all the solutions you can think of to overcome each one. You will find that when you approach goal setting in this manner, you release unexpected forces of synergy, creativity, and imagination and discover reasonable and workable solutions for any problem that might arise.

In numerous problem-solving and goal setting sessions with leaders inside our companies and leaders of client companies, we have often found that listing obstacles to a goal can provide a good list of action steps to bring us closer to the goal. For example, when we transform the roadblock "need lower production costs" into action-oriented items like "study new production processes for cost-saving aspects" or "go to more outside manufacturers for bids," we may discover a solution...or at least one action step that will help us build the momentum to reach our goal.

RANDY SLECHTA

The most critical element of the planning process is the achievement of some sort of balance between personal and organizational goals and among personal goals themselves. In the development of a personal plan of action, highly effective leaders rely on this sense of balance to guide them in the formation of goals for all six areas of life. They then balance these personal goals with the demands placed upon them by the need to achieve important organizational goals.

Just as a clear vision, mission, and purpose is necessary to crystallized thinking, so a balanced approach is vital to the success of personal and organizational goal setting.

Pillar Three: Creating Desire and Passion

The third pillar of support for the leadership bridge involves the development of a sincere desire among you and your team members to achieve personal and organizational goals. A burning passion for achievement marks the difference between a real goal and a mere wish. A wish or a daydream has no substance; it is vague, unformed, and unsupported by any action. Desire, on the other hand, puts action into the plans you've made. Without desire strong enough to produce action, you and your team will achieve little, no matter how worthy the goal nor how workable the plan you've devised.

All of us are born with the desire to achieve, but we also have endured a great deal of conditioning. Some of us may have allowed the flow of creativity and desire to be cut off by outside circumstances and influences. When we rediscover the freshness, vitality, and enthusiasm of the desire each of us possessed as a child, we are ready to achieve success.

When I think of building desire to accomplish a goal or to finish a task, I often think of Winston Churchill: "We shall not fail or falter; we shall not weaken or tire. Neither the sudden shock of battle nor the long drawn trials of vigilance and exertion will wear us down. Give us the tools, and we will finish the job."

PAUL J. MEYER

Many people spend their lives dispensing effort in "minimum daily requirements," just like a prescription for vitamins. They rarely exceed the minimum effort required to get by. Actually, leaders and followers alike have vast reserves of strength like that experienced by athletes who run until exhausted and then reach their "second wind." A sincere, burning desire for achievement triggers the willingness to capitalize on our full potential; passion propels you and your team members toward the achievement of personal and organizational goals. (While we were writing this passage, word came that Mother Teresa had died in Calcutta. She was an extraordinary example of leadership passion and energy. When she accepted the Nobel Prize, she accepted not for herself but for all the poor and hungry people who had found a voice in her efforts to end suffering.)

Successful leaders develop a genuine, driving passion for the achievement of personal and team goals. Without that passion, any leader is robbed of power, strength, and conviction. On the other hand, leaders who develop passion and channel their desire toward the achievement of individual and organizational objectives find their effectiveness and efficiency markedly increased.

Pillar Four: Development of Confidence and Trust

To continue building support for the leadership bridge, you and your team members must develop supreme confidence in yourselves and in your ability to achieve. For great leaders, nothing offers greater confidence than possessing clear-cut knowledge of planned actions and the order in which they should be taken. The mere existence of a written plan of action contributes immeasurably to your leadership effectiveness. The most important source of confidence you can have is knowing that you and your team can make the necessary internal and external changes that are needed for tangible goals to become a reality.

Many leaders experience difficulty in developing supreme confidence because they lack faith or confidence in the ability and performance of their team members. Highly effective leaders, on the other hand, understand that the process of achievement relies upon altering basic attitudes and habits of thinking. When successful leaders learn to trust their team members to perform adequately, they have mastered a key factor in putting their organization's plan into action. When you develop confidence and trust in the members of your team, you lay the groundwork for firm and unshakable confidence in your organization's ability to succeed.

This kind of confidence in your team members builds on a firm foundation of personal rapport that grows rapidly as you share knowledge and experiences with individual members of your organization. But the development of such a rapport necessarily implies that you must be personally involved with your team members. When you know from firsthand experience why a particular team member might be motivated to accomplish a particular task, you are incomparably more confident and trusting than you would be if you had merely assigned the task and walked away. Leaders can always gain that kind of after-the-fact knowledge by assigning work and watching the results. But personal experience—the kind of individual interaction that turns superficial personal knowledge into practical confidence and trust—comes only from subjecting yourself and your team members to situations that require the exercise of your full potential. Once you recognize the significance of personal interaction and practical experience, you will find that you and your followers will actually welcome even the most stressful experiences. These stressful experiences are strong builders of leadership confidence and trust.

> *Frequent personal interaction with team members serves to keep your mind focused on potentials and victories rather than on fear, doubt, worry, indecision, and negative thinking.*

Rex Houze has been sharing the four keys to trust in leadership with Leadership Management Inc. business owners for a quarter of a century. To trust effectively, leaders must know their people, know their goals, know their activity, and know their results. Anything less breeds mistrust and lack of confidence.

Each fall, I ask our business owners to write down their goals for the year to come. When I review those goals, I know what they want to accomplish. When I get to know each individual personally, I come to understand why the goal they've set is important to them. From their track record I can gauge their activity, results, and effectiveness. They know I want to help them grow their business—and I know what they want to achieve and why. It makes for a winning combination.

REX HOUZE

Personal interaction with team members reinforces your confidence and trust by providing a clear understanding of your team members' capability, of progress made, and of goals already achieved. As a result, highly effective leaders develop within themselves the attitudes of trust and confidence in their team members. Together with their followers, they begin to look for ways that things can be done instead of looking for reasons why they cannot be done.

Pillar Five: Fostering Commitment and Responsibility

The fifth pillar supporting the leadership bridge is the development of a commitment to follow through on your plan regardless of obstacles, criticism, or circumstances and in spite of what others say, think, or do. This last leadership essential sets you apart from the mediocre multitudes of leaders and managers who yield to the pressure of society, the desire for acceptance, and the temptation to conform. Ironclad commitment is not the same as stubbornness. It is, rather, the application of sustained effort, controlled attention, and concentrated energy. The development of commitment and the acceptance of personal responsibility for results are the hallmarks of your refusal to be dissuaded, sidetracked, or steered off course.

One of the techniques for developing this kind of commitment and determination is the use of the "act as if" principle. Begin to act as you will act when the goal is reached. Practice the leadership attitudes and habits you have chosen to develop. We learn to do by doing. Act out the leadership role you have chosen for yourself, and you believe in the possibility of reaching your goal. For you and your organization, the greatest motivator of all is belief.

The key to the development of ironclad commitment lies in the acceptance of personal responsibility for the success or failure of your organization...and for the achievement of your personal goals as well. All effective leaders realize that final success or failure rests largely in their hands. If success is to be transformed from a dream to a tangible reality, it is the responsibility of the successful leader to see the process through.

The Five Pillars: Ready to Build

Critical Crossroad; Key Questions

These five pillars mark the key points of the support structure for the leadership bridge. Some part of each pillar is already a vital part of your personality. Some pillars are probably already better developed than others. The bridge to leadership change is a viable pathway that helps you develop the skills of highly effective leadership as you work to strengthen and build upon each of the five pillars. And each pillar serves as a valuable template against which to measure every goal, every plan, and every activity. Whatever you and your organization plan to do tomorrow, next week, or next year, ask yourself:

- Have I crystallized my thinking so that I know where I stand now and where I want to go? Are my vision, mission, and purpose clear to me and my team members?

- Do I have a detailed, written plan to achieve each important personal and organizational goal, and is there a deadline for its achievement? Are my personal goals balanced with the need to help my organization achieve? Do my personal goals represent a balance among the six areas of my life?

- Do I have a burning desire to achieve the goal I have set for myself? Have I developed within my team members and myself a passion for achieving the success we've envisioned?

- Do I have supreme confidence in our ability to reach our goal? Do I trust my team members to strive toward success and to continue to develop more of their innate potential for achievement?

- Finally, have I accepted personal responsibility for the success of the team—and for the achievement of my own personal goals? Do I possess the iron-willed determination to follow through regardless of circumstances or what other people say, think, or do?

Use these critical questions as a template. As you begin your effort to bridge the leadership gap, they serve as a self-evaluation, allowing you to determine whether you've built a strong foundation for success.

By applying the concepts and ideas outlined in the next five chapters, you can answer an emphatic "yes" to each of these questions. At that point, you will have built the five pillars of the leadership bridge—and you will be ready to embark on a challenging new journey toward the exciting changes and achievements that lie on the other side.

The First Pillar:
Crystallized Thought

Dreams and Achievement

The Value of Crystallized Thinking

Even in the rush of day-to-day activities, the most effective leaders take time to dream. They understand that a clear and unlimited vision—the ability to see themselves and their teams accomplishing great things—is their inheritance, their birthright, and their greatest single source of inspirational and motivational power.

But a grand vision can shrink to aimless wandering without careful thought and attention. Crystallized thinking moves dreams a step farther, honing and sharpening the aims and ambitions of unlimited vision into worthwhile goals and objectives. Successful leaders recognize that these goals, crystallized and well-defined, await only careful planning and the catalyst of actual effort. As the part of the leadership equation that spans dreaming and planning for achievement, crystallized thinking is one of the most valuable leadership commodities you can possess.

The best leaders crystallize their thinking to distill their unlimited vision. Crystallized thinking helps them identify the specific goals they want to achieve...and identify where they and their team stand now in relation to those objectives.

Almost every leader and manager experiences serious moments of soul-searching. They ask themselves where they stand and where they want to go in various areas of life. But is this an exercise of unlimited vision and crystallized thinking? Usually not; these soul-searching interludes typically produce only vague, elusive answers...if they produce any answers at all.

First, Know Thyself

Clear-thinking leaders understand that developing a vision for their organization and crystallizing their thinking about goals and objectives requires first understanding themselves. The most effective leaders use crystallized thinking to determine exactly where they stand now and where they want to go. Only when leaders have examined themselves are they ready to examine and develop a course of action for their organization.

Socrates said "Know thyself." Unfortunately, his admonition failed to include specific instructions that would enable us to accomplish that feat! Because everyone's personality is complex, it is never easy for leaders and followers to know themselves. Specifically, motivation is subject to certain basic needs and drives that exert influence from within. And all of us are continually subject to many outside influences and pressures...conditioning from our family, our society, our environment, and our institutions. Still, conditioned habits of thought and action are fashioned by free choice; that same freedom of choice directs crystallized thinking and the objectives crystallized thinking will produce.

Knowing yourself and where you want to go also involves some degree of decision-making. Knowing yourself implies a certain amount of faith; there is never a point at which knowledge, information, or data is complete and totally accurate. Ultimately, you must act. Highly effective leaders use crystallized thinking to arrive at a decision...and then they act on that decision. For them, crystallized thinking is the process that makes it possible to reach confident decisions about the goals they've chosen to pursue.

Crystallized thinking is the act of clearly defining goals and objectives. If you are dissatisfied with your present rate of progress compared with your true potential for success, your goals are not clearly defined. Every achievement in leadership and in life is based upon that simple comparison. Every achievement in any area of life begins with the knowledge of current status and eventual destination.

Have you ever had a friend or relative call you from a nearby city and ask for directions to your home? If you are not familiar with the nearby town, neither of you can determine an exact starting point for directions. Before the conversation goes anywhere, one of you has to crystallize thinking about your current location so that you can find a common reference point for directions. The same holds true for your pursuit of success. You have to know exactly where you are before you can begin taking steps forward.

PAUL J. MEYER

The same sort of crystallized thinking that brings highly effective leaders in touch with themselves and their potential is also the dynamic, shaping force that determines a course of action for the entire organization. At that level, questions like these serve to clearly define vision and focus thought and attention on possibilities for achievement:

- What do we want?

- Why do we want it?

- Why do we not already have it?

- Can we obtain it?

- How will we measure it?

- Whom will it affect?

- Whom will it benefit?

- Where will it lead us?

The first question—What do we want?—helps to isolate the specific dreams and desires common to both leaders and team members. What is the reason for your striving? What is the end result you seek? This is a fundamental question that you and your colleagues must answer before you can continue to narrow vision and focus.

The second question—Why do we want it?—seeks to discern the true motivation behind those specific dreams and desires. Without this vital information, the quest for success at any level becomes perfunctory and lacks real meaning. Additionally, this question may have several tiers. Suppose, for example, that you are motivated to develop a new production line because you want to have increased product to sell. The next question presents itself: Why do you want increased product to sell? Do you desire the profit that will be made? Do you want a larger share of the market?

The third question—Why do we not already have it?—requires a certain amount of soul-searching. If a goal is manifestly important to you and your team, why is it not already a reality? Is it because you lack the skill? The capabilities? The motivation? What forces have kept you from achieving the goal before now?

Two questions cannot be accurately answered. Leaders who try to provide definitive, concrete answers to the questions "Can we do it?" and "Will it work?" are only deluding themselves and their team members. In any area of business or personal life, guarantees are nonexistent. But leaders *can* assess their present situation and the *likelihood* of future circumstances and events. This analysis points to a crucible of sorts: Leaders and team members must convince themselves that the objective before them really *is* within their reach and grasp. Thus the fourth question—Can we obtain it?—becomes a critical point that broaches either a commitment to action or reluctance to move forward.

> *All of us are motivated to do things for one of two reasons: to gain a benefit or to avoid a loss.*

The fifth question—How will we measure it?—demands some sort of accurate method of measuring success. Sometimes the method may be a profit-and-loss statement. At other times, the method may incorporate intangible elements, like team member morale or community goodwill. A measuring stick should accompany every worthwhile endeavor. Finding these accurate methods of measurement requires crystallized thinking and a willingness to think "outside the box." Unfortunately, conventional thinking often restricts leaders and followers alike to methods that may no longer apply.

Sixth—Whom will it affect? Will those affected include only team members and leaders, or will they include customers, suppliers, and members of society at large? Many leaders make the critical mistake of underestimating the impact that follows their actions and decisions.

Unfortunately, team members are seldom motivated by creating a small impact. A more significant impact can engender a greater willingness to contribute to the overall effort.

The seventh question focuses on benefits. Whom will the goal or objective benefit? Will it benefit only the leaders? Will it benefit only those who work on the project? Will it benefit only team members? Or is there some greater benefit that extends outside the walls of the organization? Like impact, benefit is a powerful motivator. Many leaders shortcut its motivating potential by limiting their sphere of benefit. Goals and objectives should be selected based on a criteria that center around benefit and impact. The larger and more widespread the benefit from achievement, the larger and more widespread the impact created.

The final question: Where will it lead us? Answering this question requires considerable leadership foresight and the ability to forecast trends and change. You may find, as you consider tracking data and trends, that the goal or objective you've focused upon will not take you where you and your team members want to go. This is important information…information that enables you to alter your course before the goal takes you someplace you didn't intend to go.

Closing the Leadership Gap with Crystallized Thinking

Organization Right? People Right?

All great leaders understand a simple truth: To get the organization right, they have to get the people right. But many leaders and managers just assume that once they themselves are "right," the organization will naturally follow a path toward stellar success.

This is a mistake for three important reasons. First, owners, managers, and leaders may be "right" themselves—that is, they may see themselves as efficient and productive—but unless they have crystallized their thinking to develop a vision for the future of their organization, they cannot achieve success equal to their potential. The Scriptures tell us that "where there is no vision, the people perish." Where there is no vision, the business perishes as well.

Once highly effective leaders have crystallized their thinking and know where they want the organization to go, they share those thoughts with the members of their team. Team members always want to know more—not less—about where the organization is going. The best leaders are always eager to provide that information.

Second, no organization can afford to remain static, repeating endlessly the behaviors that initially brought it success. Times change, people change, and the business climate changes. Highly effective leaders are prepared to welcome and embrace change—instead of trying to run away from it. It may take years—even decades—but effective leaders understand that any organization that does not change is doomed to extinction.

Third, aspiring leaders cannot minimize the purpose for which the organization exists. The notion that a business exists solely to produce a profit is dangerously shortsighted. Every enterprise must exist to serve several purposes; profit is only one of them. Each organization must also serve its own family of team members, its customers, and society in general.

But the expansion of a leader's thinking cannot stop there. All great leaders crystallize their thinking to help themselves and their teams know what they are striving to do, where the organization is going, and why leaders and team members are making the effort. Statements of mission, vision, and purpose are the hallmarks of crystallized thinking. They are the essential elements that must be in place before truly effective leadership can exist.

Developing a Crystallized Mission

For your organization, success always revolves around the progressive realization of worthwhile, predetermined goals. But before you move ahead to develop a plan of action to achieve organizational goals and objectives, first crystallize your thinking to determine your team's mission, vision, and purpose.

Whether for yourself or for your organization, a mission statement is a brief but powerful summary of your reason for existing. While some mission statements more closely resemble a textbook rather than a few sentences, they are all designed for the same purpose: to provide direction, focus, and consistency for everything you and your team undertake to do. The sheer act of crystallizing your thinking can generate tremendous excitement and enthusiasm. But those effects are temporary. Once they wear off, a solid mission statement will help keep you and your team members on track toward the objectives you've set.

A mission statement is only effective, however, if team members know and understand it! In many companies, employees never really grasp the meaning of the mission statement. In actuality, the livelihood of every member of the team depends on grasping both the words and meaning of the mission statement. If rank-and-file employees fail to understand and internalize it, it is management's fault. Indeed, this lack of understanding and singleness of purpose can eventually contribute to any leader's downfall.

Just as you and your organization have mission statements, each member of your team should have one as well. Personal and business mission statements serve as a foundation for guiding decisions, actions, and goals in both career and private life.

The "sensational" business decisions you read about in the business section of your daily newspaper are usually made by companies operating without mission statements. Because there is no crystallized thinking or grand design guiding the actions of these managers and leaders, the decisions they make are often distracting. These individuals have typically lost sight of their true purpose—both personally and in a business sense—because they haven't been able to crystallize their thinking and focus their collective creativity on unique impacts and outcomes. Their oversight detracts from—and may destroy—the contribution, impact, and success of their own organization.

Look at your own organization's mission statement. This assumes, of course, that you have one in place; if not, crystallized thinking will help you create one quickly and efficiently. If the mission statement reads more like a novel than a bumper sticker, work to make it as succinct and as brief as possible. Why? Because you cannot expect your team members to understand, accept, and internalize a mission statement that they cannot memorize. For example, Leadership Management Inc.'s mission statement—"To provide the leadership, knowledge, and other resources required to develop successful LMI businesses"—is easier to memorize than, say, an inaugural address.

A solid, concise, well-written business mission statement is the epitome of crystallized thinking. It describes the purpose of the organization in terms relating not only to product or service marketed but also in terms of who comprises the market for the product or service, how the product or service benefits the consumer, and how the business will benefit from success. Most successful leaders know they will be unable to achieve their goals unless everyone involved in the process can achieve their own goals.

In the final analysis, the input of every team member will probably be required to construct a complete, concise, well-balanced mission statement. Admittedly, you'll need patience and a good long-term perspective if you want to capture the thoughts and ideas of every member of the team, but the result is even greater dedication and involvement from every individual.

> The best leaders have learned that they cannot lead without listening.
>
> REX HOUZE

By paying close attention to team member input, leaders can chart an organizational course that will closely parallel the dreams and desires of rank-and-file workers as well as leaders and managers. The definition this process gives to the organizational culture—as well as the pride it generates—elevates the organization's ability to attract and keep good team members. Team members who are excited to "be on board" dedicate themselves to the group's mission more readily than those who are unsure that they have made a laudable career move. The inevitable result is a more closely-knit group of individuals, unified to achieve a long-range common goal and committed to the same central purpose.

Putting forth the effort required to crystallize your thinking and define the mission of yourself and your team will reward each of you with a solid, stable foundation for future achievement. Just as the strength and stability of your foundation of values determine the heights to which you and your organization can aspire, so your mission statement—coupled with your commitment to developing your team—will effectively predict the eventual success of the business.

Creating a Crystallized Vision

A mission statement tells your team members and customers what the business does; a vision statement lets them know where the business is heading. If crystallized thinking and a mission statement are critical elements in developing highly effective leadership, a vision statement should be regarded as something even more vital. For you, crystallizing your vision makes the process of becoming an effective leader much easier. For your associates, a concise vision identifies your overall business goals and links their goals to yours.

Without a vision statement, many of your team members are likely to feel that they are a part of something quite ordinary—something drab, dull, and lacking direction. The vision statement sets the tone for the future of the company. It should be exciting but brief; it should convey a sense of urgency and a clear sense of corporate destiny.

RANDY SLECHTA

As an example, LMI's vision statement is simple and concise: "LMI's vision is to be America's preeminent resource for developing effective leaders in business and industry." Every member of the LMI home office staff can quote the vision statement as readily as the mission statement.

Indeed, many LMI business owners feel that their futures are so inexorably tied to LMI's continued growth and development that they carry the vision statement with them constantly.

If you aspire to highly effective leadership, take a good look at your vision statement. If you don't have one, you need to set about creating one...today. A vision statement defines the future. Every day you work without it, you are working for yesterday rather than for tomorrow. Your vision statement should be a conduit or channel for your goals and expectations. It should challenge you and your team members to a bright new future without burdening anyone with the mistakes and poor choices that may have been made in the past.

While a mission statement is largely a consensus of crystallized thinking, a vision statement may not require input from every member of your team. If you own the business or help lead it, you are the individual who should determine—or, at the very least, help determine—what the future holds. Truly successful leaders know where the organization is headed. Their crusade focuses on leading team members along that predetermined pathway to success.

While your mission statement represents the reasons you and your organization continue to exist, a vision statement serves a higher purpose: It tells the world what you intend to do with the gifts your Creator has given you and your team members.

Inspiring a Crystallized Purpose

A statement of purpose tells the world why you and your team are making the effort to succeed.

In the greater scheme of things, a statement of purpose should probably come before mission and vision statements. After all, the motivation for action must precede the action itself. Many businesses and highly effective leaders already have mission and vision statements...although often overly wordy and imprecise.

So why save the statement of purpose for last? Largely because it requires the highest degree of crystallized thinking— this is the prime reason why most leaders and organizations lack anything resembling a statement of purpose. A statement of purpose requires deliberate, crystallized thinking aimed at answering a single fundamental question:

Why am I doing what I'm doing?

This question applies as much to you personally as it does to the organization to which you belong. It also applies to every single individual who helps you in the effort to be successful.

So, why are you doing what you're doing?

At its essence, this is a personal question; no one can answer it except you. You are infinitely more qualified to decide your purpose than anyone else. So what is your overriding purpose? Is it money? Is it your family? Are you doing it all for your team members? For your community? For society in general? For God? Only you can decide.

Your statement of purpose should be as brief and to-the-point as are typical mission and vision statements. Indeed, all three statements should require less than a hundred words. LMI's statement of purpose is this: "To enhance personal, corporate, and national productivity by developing leaders who have clearly defined goals, positive attitudes, and leadership skills, thus empowering them to use more of their God-given potential."

All told, LMI's mission, vision, and purpose statements require something less than six dozen words. On the other hand, you have probably seen companies and organizations use more than seventy words just for their mission statement. Which do you expect would be more memorable?

Crystallizing Your Team s Vision, Mission, and Purpose

A Plan in the Sand

Bill Hinson and I were walking along the beach at Ft. Lauderdale, dragging our toes in the wet sand. It was a warm summer evening in 1958. Bill was my pastor, my friend, my confidant. We were about the same age; that made it easier to share my private agony with him. For the first time in my life, I was a ship without a rudder. I didn't know what to do next. My career in the life insurance industry had made me wealthy, but that industry seemed to be headed down paths I didn't want to walk. My choice, then, was simple: compromise my values and continue to do just what I'd been doing for the past decade or find something new to which I could devote my time, energy, and conviction. "You know, Paul," Bill said quietly, "the only time I've ever seen you really happy is when you were helping someone develop and use more of their full potential for success." That was true enough. I'd found that I enjoyed selling a life insurance policy in fifteen minutes and then spending three or four hours with my new clients showing them how they could change their lives. "Why don't you start a company with that as its purpose?" Bill asked. "Easy for you to say," I replied evenly enough, unaware that my life had just been changed forever. "You're on the payroll of the church...you know where your next meal is coming from!" Hinson laughed, then grew serious again. He began to talk about a company that was using phonograph records to communicate religious messages. If that concept served as a transmitter of God's Word, why could it not also be used to help others develop the potential God had given them? That moment marked the genesis of our unique contribution to the personal development industry. While seminar speakers and books had been around for a long time...and are still around today...no one had yet created a workable method that would allow individuals to learn at their own pace, on their own time, and to develop a plan of action that would help them give direction to their dreams. And Bill was right—it would work. But I had a lot to learn first. I had to learn about the recording industry; I had to talk with successful authors about the rights to use some of their material. I had to fine-tune my concepts of spaced repetition and convenient learning. There was no one else doing what I wanted to do; I would have to invent the product, the process, and the company as well. The wheels were spinning in my head...and nearly four decades later, they haven't stopped! There was, however, one aspect of my yet-to-be-born company that was already in place...it had a purpose. From 1960 on, almost everything we produced bore a slogan: "Dedicated to motivating people to their full potential." No matter how successful our companies became, no matter how much good our programs have done for people around the globe, our purpose has never been clearer than it was that evening on the beach in Ft. Lauderdale. And Bill Hinson, who first enunciated that purpose, is still my very good friend.

PAUL J. MEYER

Crystallized Thinking and the Future

Remember: If you are not now making the progress you would like to make and are capable of making, it is simply because your goals are not clearly defined. If you want to move forward to develop your organization's full potential for success and achievement, clear and concise mission, vision, and purpose statements are essentials. They are the first step toward clearly defining the goals you and your team members wish to achieve.

These statements can no longer be thought of as buzzwords or the latest business fad. They cannot be considered the exclusive property of commercial intellectuals and business consultants. These statements should have been a part of every business enterprise since the dawn of commerce. Had they been, we would all be much more successful today.

Why? Because written mission, vision, and purpose statements crystallize thinking...just as a written plan of action does. Crystallized thought motivates action...the right kind of action. Typically, the right kind of action produces the right kind of results.

If you fail to crystallize your thinking or decide to ignore the creation of your unique mission, vision, and purpose statements, you choose to consign yourself and your organization to the dustbin of business history. Your organization and team may not collapse tomorrow, or next week, or even in the next decade. Sooner or later, though, the lack of crystallized thinking will drive you and your followers into the ground. Because you could not be bothered to think through what you do, why you do it, and where you want to take it, you will have dug the hole yourself.

A few moments of creative thinking pay huge leadership dividends. In quiet moments of solitude, leaders renew their strength. Seize this time to remind yourself of your personal and business mission, vision, and purpose.

Finding opportunities to crystallize your thinking may require pulling away from the alluring addiction of seemingly urgent tasks. You pause and refocus because you yearn for lasting achievement and significant meaningful success. Investing time and emotional energy in crystallized thinking refreshes your inspiration, motivation, and creative energy.

The Second Pillar:
Plans and Balance

The Science of Achievement

The Importance of Written Plans

The next step toward maximum effectiveness involves the development of written plans for the achievement of specific objectives…goals that move the team forward and help both leader and team members develop personally.

Just as a sprinter has a finish line to cross, so every individual—whether leader or follower—has goals to attain. The difference is the pathway to the finish line. The sprinter runs down a narrow lane, and the boundaries are clearly marked. Moving one foot in front of the other eventually brings the sprinter to the finish line. The more complex process of goals achievement, on the other hand, gives us all broader options to consider.

Written plans help determine both how and when you and your team will cross the finish line. Will you run straight down the lane to your goal? Or will you move from side to side, experiencing the path to achievement in a different way? The decision is yours, of course. Like the decisions you've made through crystallized thinking, you can't afford to abdicate your control over the process. Now is the time for the sprinter to take longer strides; now is the time for you to set forth workable plans and guidelines. Written plans are essential if you intend to push your goal beyond the realm of daydreaming. With plans clearly detailed and carefully drawn, you cut through the confusion and conjecture your own thought process may have created. Whether you consider your leadership journey a sprint or a marathon, written plans allow you to convert theory into practice, thought into action, and dreams into reality.

All successful leaders crystallize their thinking and have a clear understanding of their organization's vision, mission, and purpose.

Developing written plans carries with it an impressive benefit: The plan minimizes the tendency to procrastinate. The plan itself creates an "inspirational discontent" with things as they are. Truly effective leaders clearly visualize the attainment of the goals they set. These objectives appear to them as accomplished fact…even before they start down the road to achievement. As a result, highly effective leaders are more committed to a particular plan of action and are more confident in their ability to achieve the goal. Energy, excitement, and enthusiasm are all stimulated by written plans of action. Rather than wondering when—and if—they should start, highly effective leaders can hardly wait to begin.

Watching my mother inspired me to always have something to write on…and something to write with! Capturing a new idea, recording a thought, or outlining a plan of action on a sheet of paper or a note card is now a habit for me. Wherever I am, there are cards, tablets, and notepads. My wife says I have notepads everywhere! If you can't write something down, you can't crystallize it, and you'll probably never achieve it.

PAUL J. MEYER

Written plans for the achievement of goals contain these essential elements:

- The goal, written in a clear and concise manner

- A deadline or target date for the achievement of the goal

- A summary of benefits to be gained and losses to be avoided as a result of achieving the goal

- A summary of possible obstacles to achievement along with written strategies for overcoming these roadblocks

- A step-by-step plan for the achievement process

Putting goals on paper serves as a commitment to achievement. Successful people rely on written plans as guideposts in the quest to develop each area of life. For one to become an extraordinarily successful leader, written plans are the second essential element.

The Challenge of Balance

Exemplary leaders use written and specific goals to develop a keen sense of balance in themselves and the members of their team. The pathway to this unique sense of balance is the road to becoming a Total Person.

Every leader, to become highly effective, must first become a Total Person. As we saw in the preceding chapter, a personal purpose and direction are the first critical steps. Then come goals for six areas of life, and, finally, the balance that merges all six areas into a cohesive whole.

To become a Total Person and a complete leader, first focus on achieving your full potential as an individual. Commit to growing personally by setting and striving toward achieving challenging goals in six key areas of life: Family, Financial, Mental, Physical, Social, and Spiritual. Each of these six areas demands excellence from all of us—and each area is a benchmark of the Total Person process.

Why is it imperative for a highly effective leader to first become a Total Person? Simply stated, leaders are role models. If they overlook one or more of the six areas of life, they automatically develop something of a lopsided existence. Regardless of status or station in life, an out-of-round Wheel of Life makes for some rather painful progress up and down the hills of human experience. When leaders display a lopsided existence, the integrity of their leadership is compromised as well.

If your Wheel of Life has a flat spot...or two or three...it's likely that you have neglected one or more important areas of your existence. As a result, you're in for a very bumpy ride through life. This "bumpy ride" is responsible for most of the difficulties that plague modern society. Think about it—individuals who are deficient in one or more areas of life tend to warp and distort the other areas. Warped lives are not just created by accident or circumstance. Instead, they are the result of deliberate choice, the inevitable consequence of the neglect and abandonment of various aspects of life. The result is an out-of-round individual, someone who is out of balance and often out of control as well.

Let's examine the six areas of life that make up the Total Person:

Family—Family goals affect you and those you love. They are usually goals that guide your interaction, define your commitment, and create a cohesive sense of worth that binds you to those you care about.

Financial—Financial goals affect earnings, savings, and investments. Financial goals govern how you earn, acquire, and use financial leverage. Financial goals also relate to career advancement, business contribution, and your personal legacy to those you love.

Mental—Mental goals focus on expanding the mind. Mental goals allow you to gather knowledge that leads to improvement of your spirit and condition. Mental goals direct your quest for mastery of any subject or skill. Mental goals guide you toward intellectual pursuits and help you experience the joy of learning.

Physical—Physical goals help you improve your body. Physical goals govern the kind of physical shape you are in or wish to attain. Physical goals may also focus on recreation and sporting activities you enjoy. Physical goals deal with your overall health and fitness.

Social—Social goals strengthen your ability to interact personally with others. They help you engage in new and different experiences, meet new people, and accept new challenges to live and work with others.

Spiritual—Spiritual goals affect your relationship with your Creator. These goals bind you to whatever faith you profess. Spiritual goals create and tie you to certain ethical standards of moral behavior and conduct. Spiritual goals can help you express your own religious philosophy.

No one—regardless of lifestyle or status—can justly be considered a Total Person unless he or she has developed significant goals for each of these six areas of life. No one can become a highly effective leader without becoming a Total Person first. And no one can attain Total Person status without a clear-cut purpose or overall reason for living. The neglect of any one of the six areas—or the abandonment of purpose—leads to the abandonment of Total Person status. A balanced Wheel of Life is an essential element of lasting successful leadership.

The Wheel of Life

The six areas of life can be compared to the spokes of a wheel. Each spoke radiates out from the center of the wheel—the center of your life—to the rim. It's quite possible that, given a lack of focus on one or more areas, some spokes will be longer than others. In fact, some spokes may be quite short. Only a few spokes may actually be long enough to reach the rim.

As you might expect, spokes that don't reach the rim can create a Wheel of Life that is shaped more like a triangle or a trapezoid. A lopsided wheel—one that is not round—will not roll very fast. It may not even roll at all. This is precisely the effect that ignored areas of life have on the Total Person—they grind all forward progress to an eventual halt.

For you to become an effective leader, it's important that each spoke of your wheel—each of the six areas of life—be adequately developed. If, for example, you focus on four areas and neglect the other two, your forward progress still will be severely handicapped. Only by developing a well-rounded wheel can you be assured of making the kind of progress necessary to reach your goals, lead others effectively, and utilize more of your God-given potential.

The Result of Neglect

Regardless of their level of effectiveness, leaders are often extraordinarily busy people. Indeed, you may feel that you are already running at peak potential, that you have no more time, no more energy, no more effort to give to becoming more than you are. It is, however, a grave mistake to ignore the various areas of your life simply because you believe you cannot spare the time or effort required to develop them.

A balanced life requires attention to all six key areas...not just to two or three.

Why? First, because you have probably not yet reached what athletes call "second wind." Typically, a runner can run until exhausted. If the runner persists, however, he or she will quickly discover an untapped resource of additional energy. This "second wind" only manifests itself when the first wind has been completely exhausted.

Additionally, ignoring various areas of life—or believing that you need not devote time and attention to them—consigns you to failure in one or more other areas of life. Because you believe you are already running at top speed on the road to success, you may feel that you have nothing extra to give to specific areas of life. It's a good bet that one or two areas are already suffering the effects of neglect. The end result will be a Wheel of Life that is severely out-of-round and out-of-balance.

Most successful leaders have found that living life out of balance actually causes them to slow down because they are forced to divert their focus to problems that occur in the ignored or neglected areas of life.

If we carefully observe individuals who contribute to the continued decline and destruction of modern society, we find that they typically lack an understanding of the need to become a Total Person. Because these individuals lack goals and objectives in the key areas of life, anything approaching a balanced existence is an unreachable ideal for them.

A basic human tragedy is that most of these individuals have a severely limited belief in themselves and their potential for success. They have never taken time to examine life as a whole; never bothered to think about different areas of life. As a consequence, they have never learned the art of straightening and strengthening the wheels of their own lives. Their neglect is our neglect. Many of us have been content enough to let these individuals go their own way so long as their paths did not cross ours.

Efficient and effective leaders look for ways to make paths and human potential intersect. These crossroads are an opportunity to teach, coach, and direct. They represent every leader's best chance to help others bring out the best in themselves.

Showing your followers how to develop their full potential and create a balanced existence forges a common bond between you and other committed leaders…and between you and the members of your team. It is this process—the development of yourself and your people and the attainment of balanced lives— that is the essential element of highly effective leadership.

Where Do You Stand Now?

Your Personal Assessment

Where do you stand now in each of the six areas of life? Where do you stand in the development of a passion or purpose for living? In the early days of our companies, we provided prospective clients with a bar chart that illustrated six graph ranges corresponding to the six areas of life. The key elements of that chart are here for you to use.

Think carefully about your status in each area of life. If "10" represented perfection and "1" only minimal impact, where would you rank yourself? Where would you mark your progress in each area of life?

How Do You Rate Yourself?

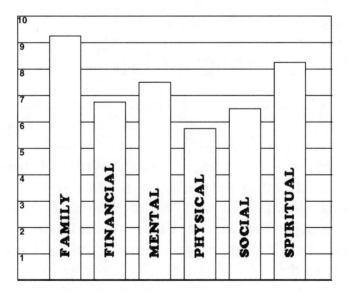

Take a few moments to think about your life as it is today. Then mark each area of life to reflect your honest evaluation of where you stand now in relation to your potential for success. Be as honest as possible...no one need see your chart but you.

Wheel of Life®

When you've finished marking the chart and are satisfied with the rankings you've assigned yourself in each area of life, take a few moments to evaluate what the chart shows overall. Which areas of life need most work? In which areas of life do you currently excel? In which area could you create the greatest immediate impact? Which area would take the most time to improve?

Now imagine that each area of life is a spoke on the wheel of your existence. How round would your wheel be? How well would it roll through life? What goals can you begin to achieve today that will contribute to a more rounded wheel?

Many leaders who have achieved extraordinary success in the business world are dismayed to see that their own self-evaluation indicates dramatic need for personal improvement. If this is true for you, you may find yourself feeling downcast, depressed, or even angry about where you stand in the other areas of life. But there's no need to feel dejected about the rankings you have assigned the various areas. Instead, turn any negative emotion into a positive, productive passion...a genuine enthusiasm for making appropriate changes.

Begin making significant changes by setting goals and priorities in each area of life. Indeed, you will find even small changes significant and exciting! Then develop the step-by-step plans designed to guarantee the achievement of those goals. Once you have the plans in place, it's time to get into action to achieve the results you want...and to cast a better-rounded Wheel of Life.

> You've heard the old saying: 90 percent of all failure comes from quitting. The obverse is also true: You are 90 percent of the way to your goal the moment you begin the quest for achievement. You begin to see improvement in various areas of life from the moment you settle upon challenging goals and commit yourself to their achievement.
>
> RANDY SLECHTA

Your conscious focus is determined by your subconscious intention. If you are sincerely focused on improving your standing in various areas of life, you find that you begin paying attention to different things. As a result, your subconscious actions allow others to see your immediate improvement as well. When those you lead see you change, your actions and behavior offer strong validity to your acceptance and internalization of the Total Person concept.

Goals for the Six Areas

An Overview

Determining where you stand in each of the six areas of life may be a slightly painful process, but it is a necessary one if you are to give direction to your dreams. The process also can be an enjoyable one as you relive and recognize the success you've achieved so far in each area. And gaining self-knowledge through this kind of self-examination process can also be extremely stimulating; you develop a well-balanced awareness of who you really are now. This is valuable information as you explore the kind of individual you wish to become.

All of us are tempted to practice doing the things we do best. This is because we all possess unique strengths and abilities that we enjoy using. However, we all have certain shortcomings and deficiencies that we often wish to ignore. As a highly effective leader, you recognize not only those talents and abilities you put on display but also the hidden weaknesses that you seldom think about or admit. Were you to continue to hide your deficiencies, they could well sabotage your efforts to become a balanced individual. Ultimately, they might affect your success and the success of those you lead as well.

When you are satisfied with the overview you've created, you're ready to move ahead to set concrete goals in each of the six areas of life. This process demands that you decide what comes first, second, third, and so on. Your own values will serve to guide you in selecting those items that will have greatest priority for you.

Once you have established priorities, you will probably be able to picture the end result of achieving the goals you have set. This is a critical litmus test; without a clear mental picture, the results you obtain will likely be blurred or distorted...much like taking a picture with an out-of-focus camera. There is no way to achieve a clear-cut goal unless you begin with a clear-cut mental picture of the result the goal will produce.

Criteria for Goal Direction

As a leader, you already know the benefits that are yours when you become goal-directed. But since goal-setting is often a generic practice, you may not be aware that the goals you set in each of the six areas of life must meet five litmus tests. If the dreams you create cannot meet each of these five criteria, they are not true goals. Odds are, they are wishes—vague and unformed to some degree.

First, goals must be written and specific. William James told us a century ago that writing crystallizes thought, and crystallized thought motivates action. If you find yourself unable to set down a goal in writing and describe it in vivid detail, then your thinking about the goal has probably not crystallized to the point of sharpness and clear definition. Hazy goals produce—at best—hazy results. Typically, they produce no results at all!

Second, the goals you set must be your own personal goals. Of course, no one else can set goals for you because no one else has your own particular view of what must be accomplished. Nor does anyone have your unique personality, your abilities, your needs, or your potential for success. Seeking goals that have been set for you by others is tantamount to pursuing borrowed goals. Borrowed goals may be positive and productive in and of themselves, but they can never generate the levels of passion, desire, and determination required for you—or anyone else—to achieve them. When your followers achieve a goal you've set for them, they feel it as a hollow victory, devoid of any lasting sense of accomplishment or achievement. The rewards mean little to them because the goal was not personally meaningful.

Third, your goals must be stated positively. While you are able to form a clear mental picture of yourself taking some positive action, it is impossible to see yourself *not* doing something! Your goals must create a vivid mental image—an image of you taking action to achieve them!

You may have noticed that those you lead often set negative goals. "I will not waste time," one person says, while another maintains that "I will not be late." Their goals would work better if you helped them state the objective in positive form: "I will make productive use of my time," or "I will arrive at the job on time."

Fourth, goals must be realistic and attainable. This is not to say that goals you set in any area of life must be commonplace or ordinary. Indeed, a mediocre goal will hold little motivation for you; a high goal is usually easier to reach than a low goal. A realistic goal represents an objective toward which you are both willing and able to work.

The attainability of a goal, on the other hand, is a question best answered by the goal's unique timetable. Long-range goals often hold less motivation than short-range goals. The key to accomplishing long-range objectives, then, is to set intermediate steps that will keep you on track and give you confidence to continue on the journey. Short-range goals, on the other hand, serve to broaden your vision. Goals that were unimaginable only days ago now move into view, and your higher vantage point allows you to see greater opportunities to express your innate potential.

Finally, the goals you set must include personality changes. This is not to say that every goal you write down must require you to change personally. Instead, you and your followers must take required personality changes into account as you plan for the achievement of specific objectives. You may find that your followers will frequently set goals to have without setting goals to become. Unfortunately, the process doesn't work this way.

All of us—regardless of level of success—must set intangible goals of becoming—of developing the required personality characteristics—before we can legitimately set goals of a more tangible nature. As you and your team members begin to work toward goals in the various areas of life, remember these five requirements:

1. The goal must be written and specific.

2. The goal must be personal...your own goal.

3. The goal must be stated positively.

4. The goal must be realistic and attainable.

5. The goal must include required personality changes.

Quest for the Total Person

The Challenge of Choices

Begin walking the path toward becoming a Total Person by first determining your most important objectives in each key area of life and then planning for the achievement of those objectives and taking daily action on your plan. Each objective is an opportunity for personal and organizational improvement, an opportunity to set and reach challenging goals that will help ensure the proper and positive development of yourself and your team members.

The first step involves assessing and reviewing strengths and weaknesses in each area of your life. Carefully examine your strengths and compare them with your opportunities to improve. Then take a moment to ask yourself another question: What one thing would I like to see happen in this area of my life?

Next, decide what comes second...and third...and fourth. Again, don't limit your imagination by taking into account the time, effort, or money required to make your vision a reality. Concentrate on making as long a list of goals as possible for each area of life.

Write down as many items as you can. You may be able to jot down only two or three ideas, or you may find that your imagination offers up an inexhaustible supply! Again, strive for quantity of items at this point. When you believe you've developed a complete list, double-check to make sure some of the items you've written down offer strength or fulfillment for some of the weaknesses you've identified.

In 1983, I gave my tennis partner and his wife one of our leadership programs. By filling out the Master Dream List in the Plan of Action, they created a list of more than three hundred things they wanted to see happen in their lives. And they did it in one weekend! When they categorized their dreams in the six areas of life, they decided that the family area had the greatest importance to them. Having a child was their most important dream. That might not sound like such a big dream, but my partner had survived a bout with cancer and a major surgery. He and his wife were sliding past the typical childbearing years. The next July, my partner and I had to forfeit a tennis match because his wife was giving birth to a baby girl. She's become the light of their lives. When you write down your dreams, you never know what will happen!

REX HOUZE

Once you're satisfied with the length of your list, give each item a reality check by working to transform it into a *SMART* goal—a goal that is *S*pecific, *M*easurable, *A*ttainable, *R*ealistic, and *T*angible. Strive to restate each idea you've written so that it meets the *SMART* goal criteria.

If an item cannot be restated as a *SMART* goal, there is an underlying reason. Is this item a mere wish or a daydream? Have you crystallized your thinking about the goal? Do you believe it's somehow unattainable? You may find that the item will forever be a vague, undefined wish. Or you may need to combat some mind-induced roadblocks that keep you from seeing your daydream or wish as a goal to be achieved.

Mental roadblocks can be acquired even at an early age. I acquired a no-limitations belief in myself and my potential while I was still a youngster. When I came home from school in the afternoons, my parents would ask me if I'd heard anything that day that would limit me in any way. I learned to be a guardian of my mind and my self-image.

PAUL J. MEYER

Your next step is to repeat the process for each of the other five key areas of life. This may take some time. Take as long as you need and avoid the temptation to rush the job. When you've begun your list of goals for all six key areas of life, you must again make the power of choice work for you.

For each key area of life, your list of goals and opportunities for improvement may be quite long, or it may contain only a single item. Most likely, each of your lists will contain several important items. Whatever the length of your individual lists, the next vital step is to prioritize the items—to decide what comes first, what comes second, and so on. Items that were previously considered critically important may need to be put on the back burner to allow for the accomplishment of another critical item. Highly effective leaders follow the habit of prioritizing goals and objectives. This is why they always know what they wish to do next after an item is completed.

From the list of priority goals in the six areas of life, create a list of things you must do today to make progress toward the top item in each area. Successful leaders strive to take positive, determined action each day to ensure that they make progress toward the achievement of worthwhile goals and objectives.

The action steps you must take today may seem small or seem relatively inconsequential. This is not a cause for concern. As long as you move slightly forward each day, you will eventually develop each area of life.

What will your action steps be today? Perhaps you'll find time to begin reading an important article in a management magazine. Or you may wish to read from Scripture or visit your church or synagogue. You may want to discuss new concepts, ideas, and events with your team members and others around you. You might have your assistant call an equipment supplier and request brochures on new machinery. Additionally, you may want to spend a few minutes catching up your checkbook or spot-checking your investments.

Whatever your goals, the important thing is to begin now. Get up and take action! Highly effective leaders *do* something daily so that the goals and dreams they cherish blossom into reality.

Where Do You Want to Go?

Your choice of goals for each of the six areas of life must be uniquely personal and based on your own value system. No one else can choose the personal goals you should opt to pursue; you must choose them yourself. Avoid agonizing over the selection of your goals; organize your dreams and desires and construct your goals from those basic elements. If you squander time and potential wondering about making the "right" choice of a goal to pursue, you will find that those who follow you will squander their time and mental energy doing exactly the same thing.

Over the last three decades, our companies have seen hundreds of thousands of clients set some extraordinary goals. We've found it helpful to provide aspiring leaders with a thought-stimulating list of sample goals…not with the idea that any goal on the list would become a part of their personal goals but, rather, to help our clients begin the thought process necessary to create meaningful objectives to pursue.

In the financial area, your goals could include:

- Earning a promotion to vice-president of the company

- Buying a luxury family car

- Increasing your income by 10 percent

- Upgrading your personal computer

In the family area, your goals might include:

- Taking the family to Hawaii for a vacation

- Moving to a larger home

- Spending more time with your children

- Enjoying a weekend away with your spouse each quarter

In the physical area of life, goals could be:

- Learning CPR

- Developing a consistent first serve in tennis

- Weighing 175 pounds

- Working out three times a week

In the social area, objectives might be:

- Joining a community discussion group

- Joining a golf club

- Meeting the parents of your children's friends

- Having a dinner party in your home

In the mental area, goals could include:

- Reading a new book every week

- Taking an advanced computer course

- Subscribing to new magazines or trade journals

- Teaching a community business class

In the spiritual area, you might set these goals:

- Providing consistent spiritual leadership to your family

- Doubling your financial contribution to your place of worship

- Developing a code of ethics with your team members

- Reading a chapter of Scripture each day

Certain goals can easily fit into two or three areas of life—they are not confined to just one. How do you know that a particular goal belongs in a particular area? You choose to put it there! Just as no one can tell you what goals to set, so no one can tell you whether a particular objective is a spiritual goal or a mental goal. That new car, for example, might be either a family goal or a financial goal…or it could be a social or mental goal. You choose where to place the goals you've set according to your own values system and your own definitions of each area of life.

The important thing, of course, is to set goals in each area...goals that will help you develop a sense of direction and fulfillment in every area of life. Don't agonize over the placement of the objectives you've set for yourself. Organize them and begin to work on the process of making them happen in your life.

Again, the items on our list of sample goals are just that...samples. They are not intended to replace your own unique personality, your own needs, and your creativity. To inspire and challenge you, goals must be personally meaningful to you—not borrowed from someone else. And, as you share the Total Person concept with your team members, make sure that the goals they set are their own goals...not yours or someone else's.

Priorities for Balanced Leaders

The Plate Spinners

Decades ago, traveling fairs and carnivals usually featured a plate spinner—someone who spun china plates atop sticks. Often plate spinners would spin five or six plates at a time, and they could keep them all spinning for hours. Of course, plate spinners learned the hard way not to pay too much attention to one plate; the others had a way of falling off and breaking if they were neglected.

So it is with your Wheel of Life. If you place too much emphasis on any one area, you risk breaking up your hard work and progress in the other areas of your existence. Being a Total Person is a bit like being a plate spinner—you must focus on all six areas at once. Paying too much attention to any one area of life can have disastrous consequences for you in other areas.

Of course, efficient and effective leaders can successfully pursue several goals at once—but they cannot try to achieve every goal they've set simultaneously. By managing yourself to accomplish, say, six to ten goals at a time, you can make sure that each area of life is well represented. You can also ensure that you do not devote too much time to any one goal or any one area of life. Similarly, you'll want to share this balancing technique with your followers. Without it, they may lead more goal-directed lives, but their Wheels of Life will remain out-of-balance and out-of-round.

Setting Priorities

Which goals will you choose to work on first? The question is most easily answered by examining your list of goals in each area of life. Select your first goals according to your own personal criteria: most important, easiest, or fastest to accomplish, and so on. Only when you choose initial goals from your list and develop written plans to accomplish those objectives can you begin to take action—action that will contribute the most toward becoming a Total Person.

The Leader as Role Model

Like Calls to Like

As you embark on the journey to become a Total Person, you will find that you take a significant step closer to bridging the leadership gap. This is because the Total Person process actually enhances the five steps to highly effective leadership. Members of your team respond to you in a new and more meaningful way because they see and sense changes in you that make you more worthy of emulation and respect.

Specifically, the Total Person process produces a rapid improvement in your own self-image...the beliefs you hold about yourself and your own worth as a leader. As you make even minimal progress in the various areas of life, you may find that you are praising yourself—if only subconsciously—for the improvements you are making. This improved self-image leads to more confident actions on your part; your ability to inspire confidence in those you lead grows as well.

Additionally, you develop a new depth of self-reliance; setting goals and making plans in different areas of life helps you deepen your self-trust. You become even more willing to commit to decisions you've made and to take the actions required to convert those choices into definitive results.

Third, developing a balanced life heightens your level of desire and initiative. As you develop goals and plans, you build an even more passionate commitment to your own future. Your willingness to change, to take appropriate risks, and to listen to new concepts and ideas grows as a result. Greater initiative helps you take purposeful action toward the achievement of the goals you've set.

Fourth, the Total Person concept inspires creativity. Indeed, no greater exercise in creativity can exist! Planning every facet of your life demands that you think "outside the box." Goal setting, by its very nature, forces you into situations in which there are no easy guidelines and few established patterns to follow. You must then devise your own path toward the achievement of your goals and your innate creativity grows as a result.

Finally, becoming a Total Person helps you become incredibly resilient. When you dare to be creative enough to plan your own destiny, you inevitably discover that some plans work while others do not. Rather than internalize disappointment and self-doubt, you can rely on your successes in other areas of life to rebound from temporary setbacks and failures. Because your creativity is in full bloom, you may find yourself devising new pathways to your goals and new solutions to the difficulties you've encountered.

Enhancing each of these qualities heightens your integrity and brings you closer to highly effective leadership. Those you lead will see you as a positive, productive role model—someone who walks the talk. Consequently, their willingness to follow your direction increases. When you share the Total Person concept with them, they readily accept your direction because they want to be more like you.

Doing What's Right

Becoming a better role model is an integral key to truly effective leadership. Your integrity calls to the integrity of your team members; the effort you are making to improve yourself and your life has a magnetic quality. It urges those you lead to make the same effort on their own behalf. The end result: You more easily encourage, enable, and manage your followers as they move through the process of becoming committed team members.

If you are tempted—by pressure, fatigue, or a slight mental letdown—to compromise, equivocate, back away, walk away, abandon, or discard an objective, remember that you are the role model your followers will emulate. Choosing to do what is right is often easier when you know that others are watching you. In this case, your followers do more than just watch; they act as you have acted. Your passion for integrity and achievement motivates you to do the right thing.

The Third Pillar:
Passion and Desire

The Fire Within

Passion, Desire, and Potential

Truly successful leaders know that the key to developing innate potential for success lies in creating a passionate desire for the development of that potential…in themselves and in the members of their team. Through crystallized thinking and the achievement of specific goals, the development of dormant potential helps leaders and team members create helpful, positive boundaries. Highly effective leaders and their followers find that they can shape their own field of endeavor merely by knowing what they want to do with it.

The way in which effective leaders utilize collective potential for success becomes the basis for their own personal and organizational integrity. On both individual and team levels, integrity is breached if potential is misused or misapplied.

"Always do right," Mark Twain once said, adding that correct behavior "will gratify some and astonish the rest." Whether you are a highly effective leader or a follower, it is far easier to do right when you have passion, desire, and a clearly defined vision for the best utilization of your potential and the potential of your team members. Doing right for yourself and those who touch your life is easier still when you have in place the crystallized thinking, goals, and plans to guide you and your team down the appropriate road to success.

Defined and refined, the goals and challenges you accept naturally create a passion and desire for success. Passion and desire manifest themselves as a thirst for excellence that will not be denied.

I'd never played tennis until I took up the game at age forty-six. I had a burning desire to become a good tennis player. I selected many role models, including Rod Laver, who was the top-ranked player in the world at that time. I took lessons from him. Then I found the player who had won more tournaments than anyone in the world—Roy Emerson. I took lessons from him. Next, I found the number one forty-six-year-old player in the world—Russell Seymour in South Africa. I took a hundred lessons from him. Then, I found the best player in Texas—Robert Trogolo—and took five hundred lessons from him. I read every single book on tennis for sale and in print at the time. A burning desire motivates you to do whatever it takes to get the job done. If I can make it work with tennis, anyone can make it work with anything, anywhere, at any age.

PAUL J. MEYER

Defining Passion and Desire

When someone achieves an extraordinary goal, we often say, "There's a passionate individual!" When someone does something that seems not to measure up to the normal standards of dedication and commitment, we typically question the individual's passion or desire for success. Passion and desire are the standards by which great leaders and followers are judged, and they are the missing elements in those who vanish with time and the tide of fortune. But why are desire and passion so highly prized, and why are they essential elements of highly effective leadership?

In reality, the notion that desire and passion are requisites for highly effective leaders is a vast understatement. Passion and desire are essential elements for *any* individual regardless of status or stature because they represent the ability to marshal human energy and potential and direct it toward maximum result and greatest good. Passion and desire are harbingers of undaunted enthusiasm and sureness of course. Passion and desire enable all of us to do what is right regardless of the personal sacrifice required or the challenge involved.

Passionate leaders see their desire for achievement as an essential extension of who they are and what they do. For the highly effective leader, passion and desire are the guiding lights that point the way toward greater success. Together, they shine as bright as beacons in the dark harbor of uncertainty, bringing inner excitement and enthusiasm to those who make decisions that affect the lives of hundreds and thousands of people. These two basic emotions and attitudes can, when properly applied, create maximum multiplication of effort for highly effective leaders and their followers as well.

Desire and Achievement

The Nature of Desire and Passion

Highly effective leaders know that talent creates its own opportunities. Desire and passion are, in a very real sense, the catalysts and developers of talent. Passion and desire combine to create their own opportunities and abilities as well. Effective leaders possess an intense, burning desire. Their passion can be transmitted to others. Desire can be learned and developed as a habit, a way of life, a deliberate choice of a living philosophy. Once ingrained in team members and leaders, a burning desire and passion to achieve become the source of new habits, new responses to experience, and new abilities.

Desire and passion are more than mere wanting or wishing, more than compulsion or stimulation. These elements of highly effective leadership represent an overwhelming inner demand for change, a personal rejection of circumstances as they are, and the willingness to make any sacrifice or bear any burden in order to bring about that change.

Desire and passion are the vital essence of a leader's inner self.

Every advance in history—in thought, in government, in ethics, art, religion, or science—has resulted from a single individual's desire to change the status quo, to win a race with time, with custom, tradition, or with self. This is why passion and desire burn like a flame in the heart of every highly effective leader. Desire is the all-important difference between winning or losing—in the Olympic Games or professional sports, the struggles of commerce and government, or a leader's quest to realize a team's full potential for greater success and achievement.

The Hallmarks of Desire and Passion

- Desire and passion are two qualities that combine to transform average executives and managers into highly effective leaders.

- Desire and passion energize highly effective leaders to keep working when problems cause other leaders and followers to give up in disgust.

- Armed with desire and passion, highly effective leaders make commitments while others make half-hearted promises.

- Desire and passion arm highly effective leaders with the judgment and courage to say "yes" or "no" at the appropriate time; those who lack desire and passion say "maybe" at the wrong times and for the wrong reasons.

- Desire and passion allow highly effective leaders to say, "I'm good, but not as good as I ought to be and will be." Leaders who lack desire and passion say, "I'm no worse than a lot of others."

- Desire and passion in team members engender respect for their leaders; lack of desire and passion can only breed resentment.

- Desire and passion instill in highly effective leaders a strong sense of personal responsibility for more than themselves; those without desire and passion typically ask, "What's in it for me?"

- Desire and passion are qualities to be highly prized by anyone who would become a highly effective leader. Desire and passion make success easier to attain and enhance the excitement of moving along the journey toward achievement.

The Results of Desire and Passion

Once internalized, desire and passion produce a certain sense of restlessness and aggressiveness. Without desire and passion, leaders and organizations are tired, apathetic, and complacent. Whether desire and passion are lost through self-satisfaction or disillusionment, the absence of these qualities reveals a barren leadership future. Why? Because a future without desire and passion promises nothing better than what was offered in the past.

Highly effective leaders who possess passion and a burning desire can clearly differentiate between mature commitment to a goal or objective and adolescent daydreaming. Desire and passion are the qualities missing in the personalities of legions of plodders and wishful thinkers. Desire and passion combine to energize leaders and followers who possess insatiable appetites for creative thinking, for action, and for achievement.

The development of desire and passion involves an active sense of self-awareness. When you know who you are and recognize the strong personal needs that cry out for satisfaction from deep within yourself, you develop an almost overwhelming sense of direction and personal purpose. You become aware that you are committed to a destiny of your own choosing; you are eager to meet and to conquer the challenges that lead to the fulfillment of that destiny.

Regardless of your current level of accomplishment, passion and desire push you to work harder. Those who lack desire often seem to be too busy to do what needs to be done. An intense desire and passion for achievement, on the other hand, point the way to exactly what is important. This is why highly effective leaders seem to know instinctively which battles to fight and when and where to compromise so they can move on to more important engagements.

Without desire and passion, on the other hand, nothing seems worth striving to attain. Among both leaders and team members, passion and desire for the achievement of organizational goals can produce a universal thirst for competition and success. The lack of passion and desire can lead to apathy and defeat.

Indeed, aspiring leaders are often surprised to learn that passion and desire force team members to analyze themselves, to look more closely at their own talents, abilities, and potential for achievement. Leaders who lack desire and passion tend to deny this introspective and competitive spirit. Typically, they devise an alibi to excuse the lack of performance from themselves and the members of their team. Others find that they have succeeded only in leveling off too soon; they must continually content themselves with less than their best.

Highly effective leaders, on the other hand, refuse to become too easily satisfied with average living and average achievements.

Developing Desire and Passion

To create desire and passion, successful leaders understand that they must challenge themselves and their team members. How individuals choose to react to a challenge determines their destiny. When do you challenge yourself? As a truly effective leader, you recognize that each new day brings with it...

- The challenge of a new opportunity

- The challenge to improve yesterday's record

- The challenge to compete against yourself

- The challenge to grow personally.

The desire and passion with which you and your team members face a challenge is an essential part of the soul of your organization. Without it, you and your team lack spiritual guidance and creative expression. Without desire and passion, there is no intuition; missing is the small voice within you to provide insight into both situations and people. Without desire and passion, all of your talents and abilities tend to lie fallow and unresponsive; your potential is hidden, buried, and dormant.

If you have allowed past leadership disappointments to destroy your passion and desire, you can rebuild even greater stores of these essential qualities. Here's a step-by-step plan for rekindling your desire and passion:

- *First:* Strive to gain self-knowledge. Examine your innermost being. Get to know yourself, your abilities, your potential, your needs. Know what excites and energizes you. Know what motivates you to take action. Crystallize your thinking and your objectives. Clarify your own personal sense of values so that you know exactly what you believe about yourself, about life in general, and about other people. Only with adequate self-knowledge can you identify the goals that will produce enough challenge and interest to create the desire and passion you must have if you are to pursue them to achievement.

- *Second:* Make sure that the goals you set, the targets you pursue, and the rewards you desire are personally meaningful. Too often, leaders and team members alike attempt to undertake projects or careers just to please parents, family, or others they admire. In the process, they deny their own natures and their own needs. Because their goals are not personally meaningful, they experience no internal desire to excel. They drift along, meeting minimum standards in positions they despise and never reach the dazzling heights to which they might otherwise have aspired.

- *Third:* Work to find wisdom and knowledge in those who are in a position to advise you. Respect their insight, their special expertise, and their superior years of experience. Ponder the advice they offer, but always remember that it is your responsibility alone to make the decisions that determine the destiny of you and your team. As much as others may care for you and wish the best for you, no one else is capable of seeing into your innermost heart to understand your deepest needs and desires.

- *Fourth:* Visualize your success. Nothing increases desire and passion for achievement like controlled and directed visualization. Something unique and amazing happens when you practice looking into the future to see yourself in possession of your goals: You become so excited, so motivated, so obsessed with desire and passion to reach them that nothing can deter you or draw you off course.

- *Finally:* Be willing to work harder than you've ever worked before. Work efficiently. Work long hours. Work willingly. No goal exerts enough power to produce desire and passion unless you are willing to invest much of your time and effort in bringing it to fruition. When you have invested a part of yourself in the achievement of some worthy purpose, your desire and passion know no bounds.

Building Team Desire

Igniting Passion and Desire in Others

Highly effective leaders are able to recreate the passion they feel—they can help their team members experience the same joy and excitement with which leaders themselves face daily challenges and opportunities. Passion and desire for success, achievement, and contribution are attitudes and emotions akin to well-directed enthusiasm. Helping your team members share the passionate desire you already feel is a vital ingredient in the leadership process. Well-directed passion and desire help you and your colleagues achieve a great deal more than people who try to work without them.

Passion and desire, like enthusiasm, are sometimes misunderstood. Many leaders and managers confuse them with the mass exuberance displayed at sporting events and political conventions. But real and lasting passion and desire do not arise from temporary animation or external excitement.

Passion and desire, carefully developed and properly used, act as emotional triggers. Essentially, passion and desire are emotion management techniques...they allow you and your team members to control the emotional climate in virtually any situation. And while it is critically important that aspiring leaders and managers possess the infinite power of passionate enthusiasm, it is also vital to bring it to bear with coworkers and team members as well.

As a highly effective leader, your personal success hinges upon inspiring, nurturing, cultivating, and directing the desire and passion of the members of your organization. Their passion and desire—like yours—are developed through a combination of attitudes and personal experience. Habits of thought and lessons learned by experience can contribute greatly to the development—or the destruction—of genuine passion.

Truly successful leaders know that the kind of effort that produces desire and passion includes working to learn skills, develop personality traits, and acquire the attitudes and habits required to achieve a specific goal or the organization's ultimate purpose. Highly effective leaders share this wisdom with their team members: Knowledge and experience come only from being active in the arena of confrontation. They never come to one who only sits and waits. To develop passion, team members must be *involved* in the process of achievement.

To foster desire and passion in team members, remind them to focus on positive personal development. Specifically, they:

- *Shouldn't bemoan their lack of knowledge.* Instead, they can study and learn.

- *Shouldn't complain that they have no experience.* Instead, begin to work out a plan of action to gain needed experience.

- *Shouldn't worry when their first efforts seem to produce only errors.* Instead, determine to try again and to make one fewer error every day.

- *Shouldn't lament the lack of opportunity.* Opportunities abound!

- *Shouldn't despair because they lack the personality traits for success.* Those traits and qualities can be developed!

True leaders know that if they and their team members are unwilling to work to achieve organizational goals, they lack passion and desire. On the other hand, when team members and leaders alike push themselves into the work, passion and desire follow swiftly.

Highly effective leaders and their team members learn to welcome the adversities of life. Each of us will know we are a real success when we can face life's tests, confront its difficulties, encounter its roadblocks, and still find the courage to continue. Ideally, leaders and followers alike should regard failure as a learning opportunity—a chance to try again and move closer to the target on the next attempt.

In the final analysis, desire and passion enable you and your team members to endure mistakes, misfortune, failure, and adversity and bounce back. If you never make a mistake or experience a failure, it is probably an indication that you are not moving forward with any degree of certainty or with any sense of direction. You have probably failed to crystallize your thinking and develop plans for achievement. You have not tested your limits because you do not know where those limits lie. Be willing to risk failure and mistakes. Each time you venture forth to face adversity or difficulty, confront it head on and dare to take action. You are stretching your capacity a little more. Of course, you will suffer some defeats. But from each one, you and your team members will learn something new and useful. Because you move a little closer to your goal with each venture, desire and passion grow and consume you.

Evaluating Desire and Passion

How do efficient and effective leaders know when they have built the kind of desire and passion that will support them in achieving their objectives?

A young man once came to the wise philosopher Socrates and asked how to attain great wisdom. Socrates took the young man down to the riverside and held his head under water until he almost drowned. When he finally released the young man, Socrates asked, "What were you thinking about while your head was under water? What did you desire?" "Air," said the youth passionately, "I wanted air." Socrates said, "When you want wisdom as badly as you wanted air just now, you will find wisdom."

RANDY SLECHTA

To become a highly effective leader, this is the kind of desire and passion that you must cultivate and develop in yourself and others. A burning desire to possess your team's goals, a passion to achieve your organization's purpose, and the overwhelming urge to help your team members reach their full potential will inspire all of you to struggle, to work, and to persevere until you succeed.

Discerning leaders can quickly distinguish real passion and desire from a mere wish or daydream by asking themselves and their followers questions like these:

- What are the obstacles or roadblocks we must overcome to reach the overall goals we desire?

- What must we give in time and effort to overcome those obstacles and obtain what we desire?

- What are the rewards we will have when we have succeeded?

- Are the rewards worth what it will cost all of us in time and effort?

If you and your team answer the last question with a resounding "yes," then you can bet that desire and passion are genuine. You and your team members will be willing to do the work, expend the effort, and invest the time required to achieve your organization's goal. You will also be willing to continually resell the members of your team on making a similar commitment of time, effort, and energy. Commit yourself to taking the necessary action, and your desire and passion will support you.

As passionate desire becomes an intrinsic part of your way of life, it begins in some strange and unexplainable way to use every circumstance, every contact, and every experience as a means to bring into reality the object of your desire. Desire and passion know no such word as impossible—they accept no such reality as failure.

Armed with passion and desire, you literally become a success magnet. The law of attraction is free to work for you. You begin to attract to you and your team whatever it is you need to be successful. Your enthusiasm electrifies everyone who comes in contact with you. Desire and passion combine to give you the extra energy and the extra determination to reach out for whomever and whatever you need to accomplish the job.

Highly effective leaders have found that burning desire and passion emerge when they begin to entertain great thoughts, great concepts, and great goals. When you catch a vision of greatness and crystallize your thinking about the goals you want to pursue, desire and passion flare into an eternal flame that warms, energizes, and empowers you.

Passion, Desire, and Rewarding Leadership

What's In It for You?

It's true. Becoming a successful leader requires a great deal of you. Nowhere is this more evident than in the development of passion and desire. Your intense effort is required to sustain the driving force of any passion, and you are ultimately responsible for the fulfillment of your desire. But the end result of your effort can be stellar success. By developing the desire and passion inherent in effective leadership, you can create a dazzling array of opportunities to bolster your personal attitude and professional success...and the success of your organization, your team members, and your colleagues as well.

What are these opportunities for achievement? First, you and your organization have the opportunity to provide a product or service that benefits others and improves the quality of their lives.

Second, you have the opportunity to command an honestly earned income that will fulfill the needs of your family and leave some money for luxuries and pleasure.

Third, as a highly effective leader, you have the opportunity to occupy a position of prominence that brings you acceptance and respect from team members, colleagues, and friends.

Fourth, you have the opportunity to feel fulfilled and complete when you have helped members of your team focus their desire and use more of their innate potential for success and achievement.

Fifth, you have the opportunity to find a deep satisfaction in facing challenging problems, dealing with fast-paced change, and overcoming daunting obstacles as you strive to reach the personal and professional goals you have set for yourself.

Sixth, you have the opportunity to experience the special fulfillment that comes from playing a significant part in the overall success of your organization.

Seventh, you have the opportunity to enjoy a special spirit of team pride when you realize that your efforts—and the efforts of your team members—have helped earn your organization the level of success it rightfully deserves.

And eighth, you have the opportunity to experience an even greater feeling of pride and accomplishment when the efforts of your organization render a significant service to your community and to society at large.

Committing to a Standard

Vibrant, successful teams *require* passionate, desire-driven leadership. The entire organization creates an internal passion and desire for success by striving for a vision, mission, and purpose bigger than itself, for crystallized goals and dreams greater and more inspiring than the mere accumulation of profit or a larger market share.

> Highly effective leaders use their passion and desire as a springboard to propel themselves and their team members to higher levels of excellence.
>
> REX HOUZE

Becoming an effective, passionate leader means deciding to use your potential for success and achievement—and the innate potential of your team members—as a force for worthwhile contribution and continuous improvement. Just as you have already experienced the never-ending challenges and opportunities inherent in growing personally, so highly effective leadership gives you an unparalleled opportunity to maintain your personal and professional integrity while you contribute substantially to the lives of other people.

Highly effective leaders guide their organization through a maze of challenges, changes, and choices. It is their passion and desire that are a constant source of energy, inspiration, and direction. But sincere desire and passion are always subject to proof: To achieve the maximum degree of team productivity, highly effective leadership and passionate desire must be as evident to team members as it is to leaders who profess to practice it.

7

The Fourth Pillar: Confidence and Trust

Self-Confidence and Trusting Others

The Dynamics of Trust

Great leaders are where they are and who they are because of the thoughts that dominate their minds—no more and no less. Confidence and faith in their own ability to innovate, develop, persevere, and succeed are key requisites in the success journey of any highly effective individual. But the leadership of others implies a wider application of confidence and trust...both of these key attitudes must be extended to encompass and empower those who contribute to the overall success of the organization.

Highly effective leaders rely on self-confidence and self-trust; both attitudes are their stock in trade. Developing and sharing that confidence with other members of the team, however, can be a daunting challenge. Why? Because developing team confidence—and confidence in the team—requires the creation of a unique and powerful motivational climate. Successful leaders strive to develop the trusting and empowering attitudes and habits that are the basis for this climate. These are the first steps toward building confidence and trust among members of the team. Truly effective leaders empower their people through a relationship built upon trust and confidence.

Unfortunately, many leaders are unable to "let go" enough to develop adequate confidence and trust in the people they manage. Others are able to delegate responsibility, but they fall short of providing the authority required to carry out the assignment. The most effective leaders, in contrast, are always seeking ways to enhance the capability, credibility, and potential of team members; the exercise of trust is an integral part of that effort.

Becoming comfortable with the attitudes of confidence and trust is not an easy process for many leaders. People who start or manage a growing business are often forced, at first, to do almost everything personally. There is simply no one else to help. But the day finally comes when that individual possesses neither the time nor energy to do everything. By bridging the leadership gap, leaders discover a way to grow and move forward. Through the development of confidence and trust in their team members, effective leaders can multiply their own efforts again and again.

> *The extension of a leader's confidence and trust marks the ultimate extension of leadership ability.*

Unfortunately, many leaders confuse the development of confidence and trust with the routine practice of delegation. While delegation is typically task-oriented, trust and confidence are uniquely people-oriented. This is not to say that delegation and follow-up are misplaced; confidence and trust, like many other aspects of committed leadership, do have boundaries. Because every leader is ultimately responsible for the overall effort of the organization, each must still maintain adequate control over each phase of the operation. Trust and confidence do not allow leaders to abdicate that responsibility. Remember, if something is important enough for you to feel that you must trust someone to accomplish it, it is also important enough to require your inspection and follow-up.

But does "inspecting what you expect" work to obliterate confidence and trust? Not at all—assuming that you control the *result* rather than controlling the team member. Through the development of your own trust and confidence, your team members develop their own sense of initiative and personal responsibility. Their passion for the work increases as well, and their respect for you grows because you have shown them that you have faith and confidence in their potential and ability.

Team members who deserve and demand your trust and confidence typically operate toward the same kinds of clear-cut objectives you have created for yourself and the organization. These objectives are opportunities for team members. They offer both an exciting challenge and a chance to make a valuable contribution to the overall effort. As a highly effective leader, you can express genuine confidence and implicit trust in each team member's ability to perform successfully. You may even offer to teach a particular process or procedure first before gradually letting go of the work. In this way, trust and confidence work together to allow highly effective leaders to take a different approach toward the achievement of the overall objective. The different approach is called *empowerment*.

Empowerment and Levels of Trust

As you develop your leadership role, make every effort to offer trust to virtually every member of your organization. Trust is the key to personal empowerment; if you withhold it, you hamper that individual's ability to grow and develop personally. If you have a legion of team members waiting to do something until you give them explicit instructions, you waste both your time and the potential of the team.

Trust and confidence, on the other hand, empower team members to seek your direction or approval and then proceed with the task. Your ability to communicate objectives and clarify assignments—coupled with your inspection of the work and a rudimentary tracking system—will go a long way toward helping team members take action and routinely report to you with their results.

The best leaders develop trust in their team members by tapping into the attitudes and values of each individual. This is the key to nurturing commitment and accountability in the goal directed team. How your team members view their work produces a significant impact on long term productivity and offers you important feedback about the individual's ability to perform to your expectations.

Confident leaders can boost their level of trust by adopting attitudes conducive to organizational productivity. Thinking and talking in terms of "we" or "us," not just "me," is a good start. Effective leaders should also recognize that mistakes are simply a part of the learning process; they imply nothing about the value, worth, or potential of the team member responsible. Indeed, leaders who recognize that team members learn through mistakes and repetition will often replace the word "failure" with words like "learning experience" or "trial."

Additionally, the most successful leaders are always available for their team members. Effective leaders offer credit for contributions to organizational success and help devise ways to keep problems from recurring. Their willingness to trust the members of their team sends an important message: "Do whatever it takes to get the job done. I'm confident that you have the talent to succeed!"

> One of the nation's biggest airlines recently embarked on a massive empowerment campaign. Employees were told to use their best judgment and do whatever it took to ensure every customer was satisfied. Legendary levels of creativity and service were the result. Witness the lady who checked her dog as luggage. At her first stop, workers transferring baggage from the cargo hold noticed that the dog was dead. Not wanting to just send the dead dog on to the lady's destination, a baggage handler replaced the animal with a nearly identical dog he'd seen at a nearby pet store. When the woman arrived at her destination, she picked up her luggage and pet carrier. She looked inside at the dog and began crying hysterically. An airline employee tried to comfort her. "What's wrong, ma'am?" he asked. The woman replied, "When I checked him in at the beginning of my trip, my dog was dead!"
>
> REX HOUZE

Many effective leaders will not always trust that each task will be completed to perfection in a timely manner, but they *do* always trust every team member to develop and use more of their unique potential for achievement.

Developing the Potential of Team Members

The Process of Learning

If leaders are to develop their own levels of team member trust and confidence, understanding how their team members grow personally is essential. Personal growth and development is more than the mere process of learning; it implies expression of new knowledge and skills in the quest to achieve a worthwhile goal. While your team members may express acquired knowledge in many different ways, the process of gathering and expressing new concepts and ideas is quite straightforward, and it applies to virtually every member of your organization. Simply stated, individuals absorb new information, tailor it to fit their own preconceptions, and express it in a way that fulfills their own needs…and the needs of the team as well.

This means that knowledge, behavior, attitudes, and values are all acquired through a process we described years ago as "mental osmosis." Of course, people are not born with ingrained or specific attitudes; those habits of thought are caused, created, and instilled by outside forces. From the moment of birth, all of us engage in a process of acquiring information, relating that information to our environment, and expressing newfound concepts and ideas to others around us. As a consequence of the information we absorb, we develop and change our attitudes and behaviors. By adulthood, our attitudes—toward life, toward work, toward other people—have largely shaped our values…the standards by which we judge the people and events that surround us. And, by the time we reach adulthood, our behavior is controlled largely by habit. In fact, nearly all daily adult activity is performed via habit.

If leaders at every level wish to develop a high level of confidence and trust in the attitudes and work habits of their team members, they must first offer new and personally meaningful ideas and information, help team members relate these new concepts to their own situation, and work with team members to develop new habits and attitudes that incorporate the new ideas.

How do team members decide what information to absorb and retain? How do they determine what they will pay attention to? Both knowledge and intelligence are acquired through a process involving curiosity and interest. Small children are fascinated by virtually everything; they acquire knowledge and information at a phenomenal rate. But curiosity wanes as youngsters move through the first years of the educational process. Finally, it becomes difficult—if not impossible—to interest a young person in any given subject. This is because their curiosity has largely been destroyed by the need to conform to the standards of the society into which they are attempting to integrate themselves.

This need to conform also helps shape and determine adult behavior in the world of work. Behavior is the recurring inclination to react in a certain way each time one encounters a particular circumstance or situation. Individuals often allow old behaviors to limit their progress purely because they do not recognize or realize the limiting nature of the way they act...or because the behaviors are comfortable and thus discourage growth and change.

Before I joined SMI, I was a teacher and coach. Working with teenagers, we tapped into the powerful urge to conform. A few young leaders on the team or in a class could greatly influence their peers toward achievement. I've found the same thing is true in the world of business. From the time I joined SMI, my leaders and mentors in the business—Paul Meyer, Joe Baxter, Ferrell Hunter, and others—have worked to create an environment of learning that helps us all stay on the cutting edge. Recently, Paul has encouraged me to lead executive book studies and learning days. By creating positive peer pressure and tapping into the adult need to conform, we have created a more stimulating and challenging learning environment.

RANDY SLECHTA

Unfortunately, the lack of conformity in team member behavior tends to destroy the trust of even the most effective leader. If the need to conform is too strong, individuals cannot grow. If it is not strong enough, chaos reigns rather than order. To establish the correct need to conform, highly effective leaders offer new attitudes, new values, and new, easily assimilated behaviors.

Habits of Thought

Like ingrained behaviors, attitudes are habits—habits of thought. They are formed in the same way as habits of behavior or action. When a particular type of thought or thought pattern gives you some sort of mental satisfaction, you repeat it. Eventually, it becomes a habit of thought—an attitude.

Attitudes are thoughts that, through repetition and the process of visualization, have become ingrained in the mind of the individual who holds them. While behaviors—habits of action—are usually formed by attempting several different courses of action and then choosing the most satisfactory one, attitudes tend to require more concrete footing. We all test habits of thought by mentally associating ourselves with past experiences. In similar situations, we are able to recall the thought almost at will and repeat it again and again.

Congruent Values

Attitudes are formed and rest upon a foundation of values. Our values determine what we pay attention to; they dictate our habits of thought. It is difficult—if not impossible—to change someone's attitudes without first restructuring the values that are essential building blocks of those new attitudes. Preconceptions and experiences of early childhood contribute to value formation. Attitudes are then tightly tied to the values that are at the deepest roots of our being. Uprooting old values in an effort to "trade" for more appropriate values requires us to first address the underlying conditioning. Unless new conditioning replaces the old, values will typically remain the same.

For decades, leaders have expected followers to magically develop value systems congruent with their own. Leaders and managers have tried to create new attitudes through efforts to educate followers and change their behavior. The vital missing link—values—has been largely ignored.

The reason is simple: Many leaders have been trained to look for the quick fix. By easily modifying how someone acts within the organizational setting—or by modifying the organizational setting itself—leaders expect to modify that individual's value system. But while behavior may be altered and knowledge augmented, values and the resulting habits of thought typically remain the same. Until the core values are changed, the attitudes remain largely inflexible. In the final analysis, long-term change never really takes place.

The most successful leaders are able to engineer value changes by helping their team members develop new, more positive conditioning and attitudes about themselves, their colleagues, the organization, team objectives, and society in general. This new conditioning, once ingrained, builds the altered value systems that produce and spur self-motivation and other productive habits of thought. Values inevitably change as attitudes and conditioning are transformed. The most significant transformation takes place as the team member acquires a more positive self-image. That self-image, in turn, is recreated again and again through the development of trust and confidence. This entire transformation is a result of effective leadership and the process of helping each individual to become an increasingly effective team member.

The Dynamics of Personal Development

The Results Continuum

Understanding how your team members grow and improve brings to light something called the *results continuum*. Put simply, the continuum serves as a schematic, or template, for accomplishment at any level. Just as attitudes cannot be altered without first changing the underlying values, so the results all of us seek are dependent upon specific action. Action is driven by habits of thought, and habits of thought are created via specific input.

In fact, any result begins with some kind of *input*. Curiosity is aroused, knowledge is shared—something must go through the mental process before any viable result can be produced. This means that the input must be mentally invigorating—it must stir something in the imagination or in the spirit that brings the mechanism of conscious thought into play.

Input comes from both without and within. In most work situations, input is directed to the individual from others on the team or from someone in a position of leadership or management. Leaders and managers require input as well, but typically they have fewer people to offer it. This means that leaders probably tend to create more mental input on their own since it does not come from someone else. Like the development of behaviors and attitudes, every individual produces some of his or her own mental input. However, acquiring the ability to produce your own input and block out the negative input of others can take time and practice. You may have discovered this fundamental truth yourself!

Positive or Negative Input?

The ideal input, from the perspective of a successful leader, revolves around goals and objectives that will contribute to the development of each team member. Effective leaders strive to ensure that the majority of the input they offer focuses on the attitudes and values conducive to the development of goals in the various areas of life. Unfortunately, many leaders are—often of necessity—too focused on immediate results and short term goals. And, as a result, they offer input that deals almost exclusively with behavior modification and skill—or task-oriented information. Any real input dealing with the team member personally is scant at best, totally absent at worst.

This is because many leaders and managers have become susceptible to negative input—*any* negative input—from other people. This tendency manifests itself in the negative way they deal with the members of their team. Highly effective leaders, on the other hand, recondition themselves and their attitudes to become perceptive to the positive input of other people. These two simple definitions understate the importance of focus and attitude; properly conditioned leaders continue to discover that the difference between the two extremes can be staggering.

If effective leaders are to build effective organizations, they first are required to accept the fact that skill building and task-oriented input will produce mostly superficial change and almost no visionary or substantive result. Successful leaders, then, strive for long term change by providing input that will help each team member continue to develop and grow personally.

Input, generated by whatever form, produces conscious thought. Thought is the basic building block of actions and results. Seldom does anything happen without conscious thought. Of course, we've all heard stories of heroic feats performed without the hero having given much thought to the task. Someone who lifts an automobile off of an injured person can hardly be expected to be thinking about the process beforehand. Indeed, in such circumstances, thinking ahead of the task would probably rob the individual of the ability to perform it. Such occurrences are the rare exception; in almost all situations, conscious thought is required before action can take place. And, just as investment precedes dividend, action is the precursor of results.

Getting Results

Action is the required element in the results continuum... nothing happens without it. It is entirely possible for someone to receive input and generate thought without taking action on the thought...in leading and managing people, you may see this happening on a daily basis. To generate action and produce an appropriate result, both input and thought must be sufficient to blast the individual out of the lethargy that is the natural product of mental or physical inactivity. A law of physics comes into play here: The body or mind at rest tends to stay at rest. Unless the input and the thought process work together to prod the individual into action, a result is never generated.

Does this mean that the result should no longer be considered the be-all and end-all of any process of achievement? Yes and no. The result is certainly manifestly important because nothing happens until some result is produced. But the process of *creating* the result can give leaders powerful insight into just what is required for the processes of achievement and self-improvement. The real benefit of the *results continuum* is to teach us all about the steps we must take before we have a legitimate right to expect specific outcomes.

Needs Fulfilling Needs

Infinite Resources, Infinite Needs

In an ordinary organization, needs beget needs. In a highly effective organization, needs fulfill needs by enlisting the untapped potential of team members. On the surface, however, this seems paradoxical at best. How can a need—a want or a desire—actually serve to fulfill another need? The answer—and the search for the answer—lies in the desire of people to become more than they are, and the striving of each individual on your team to contribute to both their individual goals and the overall objectives of the team at large.

Think for a moment about how needs beget needs in an ordinary organization. The need for more office space creates the need for more expansion capital. The need for expansion capital begets the need for additional product sales. The need for more product sales spurs the need for more production. The need for more production fosters the need for more efficient and effective workers. Needs give birth to other needs in a never-ending cycle of progress, growth, and change.

But most effective leaders recognize that resources are infinite. Workers, in an effort to fulfill their own needs and the needs of the team, have the potential to increase their production. Salespeople have the ability to increase their sales—after all, they have more product to sell. Increased sales produce a surplus of expansion capital, and some of that money can then be used to develop additional office space. The process continues, *ad infinitum*, purely because we think about the prospects of plentiful surplus rather than dwell upon limitation after limitation.

This critical attitude—this "no-limitations" habit of thought—is the second essential building block for highly effective leaders and the effective organization. Leaders who lead with an expectancy of limitation will always fail because the needs they create and dwell upon only create additional needs. If your company is in debt, for example, focusing your thought on the debt will only fasten your debt more tightly to you. Dwelling on negatives, failings, and lack will never improve the situation you face—a different habit of thought is required.

> Leaders who manage with a no-limitations belief in themselves and their people will find that the needs they help create do indeed fulfill other needs. The process moves from a chain of distraction and dissatisfaction to one of contentment and ever-expanding prosperity. Focusing on the possibilities—on what we call "possibility thinking"— allows leaders to use a need itself to point the way to solutions. This is the essence of needs-directed leadership.
>
> PAUL J. MEYER

Seeing the positive nature of needs fulfilling needs may well be the ultimate test of effective leadership. Few ordinary leaders and managers can see the needs of their organization in anything but an ambivalent or slightly negative light. Their myopic vision is induced by pressure to produce and provide for the needs themselves. Highly effective leaders, on the other hand, work to transmit the positive expectancy of needs fulfilling needs to each member of their team. A pervasive needs-fulfill-needs philosophy clearly defines—and immeasurably strengthens—the attitudes and values of the effective organization.

Effective Team, Effective Organization

What team member needs can an effective organization fulfill? In the family and home area of life, the team can offer support, counsel, and camaraderie. For goals dealing with finances and career, the organization offers the opportunity to advance in rank and position and to grow financially. In the spiritual and ethical areas of life, members of the organization can gain comfort and spirit-filled kinship from like-minded individuals. Socially and culturally, team members may provide friends, companions, and individuals with whom to share some of life's pleasures. In the mental and educational area, the organization provides opportunities to learn and grow—even if only to acquire a new skill. For goals in the physical and health area, the organization can offer some sort of health care program or insurance, and committed leaders can help team members in their quest to achieve challenging physical goals.

Indeed, it's fair to say that teams and organizations which do not support team members' personal goals actually create unfulfilled needs among those individuals. This is the central reason why workplace environments continue to deteriorate—the cause of declining productivity and abysmal morale. Until leaders take the time to become whole themselves and to establish some semblance of an effective organization, needs go unfulfilled. The end result, of course, is more of what we have become accustomed to seeing in the workplace…and continued deterioration of our enterprise, our community, and society.

Confidence on the Leadership Bridge

The Quest for Belief, Confidence, and Trust

If you wish to bridge the leadership gap effectively, and you recognize that you can attain that status only through confidence in yourself and belief in your team members' abilities, then your path is set. Becoming a confident, trusting leader takes time, because learning to have confidence and trust in yourself and others is not a rapid process. In the instant-gratification, quick-fix world that is modern management, you may feel that developing confidence in your team members is a task that can be postponed; after all, trust can wait.

Unfortunately, it does not work that way. You cannot propose to help others climb to the pinnacle of personal and team success if you are unwilling to increase your own ability to trust them. Your effort to transform others without transforming yourself is largely tantamount to going back to somewhere you have never been. Most likely, you will succeed only in destroying the vestiges of confident, trusting leadership you have already worked hard to create. Your team members will lose their belief in you, in your integrity, and in your ability to effectively lead and manage them to greater achievement.

Confident, trusting leadership is no management fad; it is a way of life. It may take you a hundred days...or a thousand... but you must strive to make trust and confidence in others an integral part of your personality before you can inspire or require it in someone else.

Developing the Highly Effective Team

You are an effective leader when you have successfully developed an effective team—a group of followers comprised of individuals who, like you, are actively pursuing objectives in all areas of life. Building your effective team will take time. How much time the process will take depends largely upon how many team members you lead, how quickly you can develop your own trust and confidence, and how intensive you choose to make the process of personal growth and organizational achievement.

When does the effective team cross the line to become an effective organization? There are really three answers—three litmus tests—that apply to that question. First, an effective organization is developed by effective work teams—note the plural form! Each team within the organization must be made up of individuals who are committed to growing personally—and to growing the organization as well.

Second, an effective team becomes an effective organization when the team members begin to give something back to the community they share and inhabit. Every community has specific and immediate needs—needs that can be fulfilled by members of the effective team. Effective teams are staffed with members of the organization who themselves have a need to make a contribution—a need that is usually fulfilled by giving something back. Your effective team crosses the line to committed organization status when they begin to contribute something to others, to organizations, and to the common welfare.

Finally, an effective organization is born when members of effective teams are convinced enough of the validity of leadership that they are willing to openly declare their trust, respect, and admiration for effective leaders. This doesn't mean that your team members must worship the ground upon which you walk...far from it. All of us have feet of clay; none of us is perfect. But your quest to become a successful leader is incredibly shallow—and probably less than genuine—if your team members cannot come to respect and admire you for your willingness to pursue objectives in all areas of life. You may believe that nothing can engender that kind of appreciation and goodwill among those you lead; you are probably selling yourself short. Heretofore, members of your team may not have expressed those qualities because they did not believe you were sincerely interested in their welfare and improvement...or that you had confidence and trust in their ability to succeed. In the process of becoming a highly effective leader, your faith and trust go a long way toward eradicating that attitude.

Remember Spartacus!

Can you measure up to the standards of a worthy leader? There is one way to find out—you can strive to emulate someone who undoubtedly *was* a trusting, confident, and worthy leader. In fact, it could be argued that Spartacus's followers died to prove his leadership status!

Perhaps you know the story of Spartacus. As a young adult, he was the leader of a band of robbers, hardly an appropriate occupation for a highly effective leader! He and his followers suffered the misfortune of being captured and sold to a gladiator trainer. In 73 B.C., Spartacus escaped and took about seventy followers with him. They hid in the crater of the volcano Vesuvius, and hordes of runaway slaves joined the band.

Spartacus became the leader of a great insurrection of Roman slaves, and he and his band eventually took control of much of southern Italy. Rome sent army after army against him, but Spartacus defeated the legions. His concern for his followers was the stuff of legend. He was fighting for a better life for them all, but it was not to be.

In 71 B.C., two years after the rebellion had begun, the Roman Emperor Crassus managed to crush the insurrection, and Spartacus was killed in a last great battle. But the Romans didn't know Spartacus was dead; they believed the slave leader was still alive and hidden among his followers.

Without exception, every follower of Spartacus took up the mantle of their fallen leader. In response to intense Roman questioning, each former slave proudly proclaimed, "I am Spartacus!" The Romans had no way of knowing who among the hundreds of slaves was telling the truth...and who might *be* Spartacus. Frustrated and enraged, the Romans crucified them all.

What if the Romans came knocking at your door today? How would your followers respond? Would they betray you and your mission? Or would they respect you enough and believe in your cause enough to risk something of themselves in your name? When you can have sincere trust and confidence that your followers would unhesitatingly make a personal sacrifice in your behalf, you will know that you have built a solid bridge across the leadership gap.

8

The Fifth Pillar:
Commitment and Responsibility

Developing an Iron Will

Developing Commitment to Goals

Here's a simple formula that can eliminate 90 percent of all the failures you and your team members will ever experience: Don't quit! Quitting accounts for the vast majority of failures to reach a particular objective or to achieve a meaningful goal.

Unfortunately, the individuals on your team who give up or quit trying are typically just as capable as you or anyone else. They lack just a few important success attitudes that can actually be cultivated and acquired quickly and easily.

It stands to reason that most individuals who give up before achieving a goal lack a white-hot, burning desire to succeed. The intensity of that desire, in large measure, determines the effective boundaries of an individual's potential for achievement. The greater the desire, the greater that individual's success potential. Desire is a jealous suitor; it leaves no room for thoughts of quitting.

You have already learned that to cultivate desire in your team members you must build upon the first few pillars of the leadership bridge. Crystallized thinking is the first essential element of desire. Unless goals are the product of crystallized thinking, it is all too easy for a team member to give up and quit at the first hint of trouble or difficulty. Intense desire cannot be aroused and created unless goals have been clearly defined.

Of course, hazy goals lack the sharp focus that allows you and your team members to concentrate your full attention and energy on their achievement. Unfocused concentration does not make someone efficient in a number of different areas; instead, it serves to add an element of mental confusion. The inevitable result is a diluted, dissipated personal power and a random scattering of personal energy.

Even those leaders who have an abundant desire to bridge the leadership gap may find themselves quitting or giving up if they lack commitment. A three-word definition for commitment: *It is done.* Commitment focuses any leader's entire being—the entire personality—on the goal that must be accomplished. Commitment is the measure of your team members' willingness to keep working toward specific goals regardless of the inherent difficulty of the task and heedless of the obstacles that they may encounter along the way.

In a way, modern technology has done us a disservice by teaching us to expect everything to be instantly available. We buy ready-made clothes, eat precooked frozen food, and sip easy-open cans of soft drinks. Even our computers run standardized and prepackaged system software. Because we have become accustomed to instant gratification for many of our wants and desires, many of us tend to become mentally upset if that pattern of immediate gratification changes.

This is the core reason behind the willingness of many people—perhaps some of your own team members—to give up at the first sign of difficulty or delay. Fortunately, effective leaders know that important goals cannot be achieved instantly...they require time, planning, effort, and dedication. Commitment is the required element for any situation that is massive and complicated, that requires the cooperation and participation of other team members, and that may not be particularly easy to achieve.

Giving up quickly is the worst possible tragedy. Leaders at every level must understand that they cannot allow lack of patience, persistence, or commitment to be responsible for missing the achievement of an important goal or objective.

The reality of the situation is this: Whenever you encounter a difficulty or a problem in the pursuit of a goal, you are free either to keep working toward the objective or to quit. Your team members, whether you realize it or not, have the same choices. Those who want to succeed—the real winners among your colleagues—will never abandon the goal no matter what happens. They will stay with the task, remaining faithful to your purpose no matter how much work or hardship is involved and no matter what other team members might say, think, or do.

Developing Persistence

The desire to succeed and the commitment to reach significant goals combine to create persistence. Persistence, over time, makes the difference between winning and losing, between success and failure. One part of persistence is raw determination, the refusal to give up, to quit, or to be defeated. Determination is a result of the confidence created by written and specific goals. Individuals who lack a detailed understanding of where they want to go and why never feel secure about their goals. Because they have failed to fully crystallize their thinking, they never really know whether the goals they've chosen are even correct! Armed with a clear, concise plan of action, effective leaders and team members feel secure enough to push ahead. They know their efforts will pay off handsomely in the end.

Patience is another key to persistence. Patience is the willingness to keep at a job, task, or goal despite temporary setbacks and encroaching difficulties. Mature people are usually willing to work now in exchange for a future reward. That is why many leaders and team members are able to work toward an important goal over a long period of time. They receive their present satisfaction—the mental reward that motivates them to keep on going—through their anticipation of the actual reward that follows. In a very real sense, persistence *requires* patience.

Leaders who have crystallized their thinking and developed written plans for the achievement of their goals find that persistence is a natural consequence of the planning process. That's because no goal, no matter how massive or minute, can be accomplished in reality before it has been accomplished mentally.

A third integral element of persistence is pride. Leaders and team members who accomplish significant goals feel a justifiable sense of pride when they use more of their full potential for success. They refuse to wait for others to push them into the limelight of success.

Of course, this kind of pride is unrelated to the boastful arrogance often displayed by those who substitute words for actions. For you and your team members, pride in winning manifests itself as a quiet, internal satisfaction in knowing that each of you has contributed the best effort possible and that the resulting achievement is both significant and worthwhile.

Persistent leaders and followers alike are willing to take appropriate risks in order to ensure the achievement of their goal. Despite your best efforts to crystallize your thinking and develop a plan for success, it is not always possible to predict with surety the end result of a particular course of action. Willingness to take appropriate risks is manifested in creativity...leaders and team members alike apply imagination and ingenuity to devise new solutions to challenging problems.

Winning leaders and their team members possess the courage necessary to attempt previously untried solutions. Those who like to "play it safe" are undoubtedly missing opportunities to move toward their goals.

The development of persistence—like any other success quality—is a little like becoming an alcoholic. Taking many separate drinks can eventually produce an addiction to alcohol that seems almost impossible to break. Just as the alcoholic must have another drink, so one who has tasted the wine of success once must taste it again...and again. Successful thoughts and actions are just as addictive as the more negative aspects of our society. Incidentally, have you ever really tasted the wine of success? It is the nectar of the gods...and you can experience it anytime you are working so hard that you do not have time to wipe away the perspiration that forms on your upper lip. Lick it off instead...and taste one of life's greatest pleasures.

PAUL J. MEYER

Finally, persistence becomes a habit of thought through the continuing practice of the attitudes and behaviors that lead to success. With enough repetition, the attitude of persistence becomes almost automatic. Those who have acquired a persistent attitude in this way seem never to think of giving up. Somehow, they automatically keep on going...and going...until the particular goal has been achieved.

In the final analysis, persistence is born of crystallized

thinking; it is created through a clear knowledge and understanding of specific goals to be achieved. Persistence grows by building another pillar on the bridge to leadership success—the written, detailed plans for achievement of the goals. And persistence requires desire and confidence. But most of all, it demands a commitment—you must commit yourself to the attainment of your objectives. When that commitment is so strong that you adamantly refuse to quit, you build rugged determination in yourself and your team members. Determination gives you and your followers the staying power necessary to stick to a chosen plan of action. And determination allows you to focus effort and energy on momentum and the achievement of the goal.

Finding Uses for Adversity

Many leaders and followers buckle quickly under the onslaught of adversity. They lack true staying power; even though they possess tremendous potential and challenging dreams, they give up and quit when difficulties arise. But successful leaders and their team members are often thankful for adversity because in every adversity is the seed of a greater or at least equivalent benefit.

Effective leaders rely upon adversity to call up the best that is within them. When you face adversity, determined to conquer and overcome it, you are literally forced to use more of your full potential for achievement. Using your vivid imagination, you develop new strategies for overcoming problems and reaching your goal. Your efforts intensify because you begin to exercise an even greater level of personal initiative. Adversity is the ultimate act of disclosure; it reveals to you the full depth of your potential, the full force of your power, and the broad spectrum of your talents and abilities.

Adversity, difficulty, and temporary defeat are stepping stones in disguise...stepping stones to greater success and achievement. Problems or setbacks cause effective leaders to react in new and different ways. These individuals also grow personally at a faster rate than might be possible were circumstances easier. The best leaders among us are sincerely grateful for the obstacles that serve to test the commitment of themselves and their team members and for the difficulties that demand the best of every member of the organization.

A Problem-Solving Plan

All leaders face difficulties, and, at some time or another, all leaders become discouraged. Instead of giving in to difficulties and discouragement, I've developed a plan for handling the problem. First, I write out a list of four or five reasons why I'm thankful that I have been given the problem. Of course, this requires some degree of persistence; thinking of five reasons for being thankful for adversity isn't always easy to do! My list might include reasons like these:

- I'm thankful I did not face this obstacle five years ago when I didn't have as much knowledge and experience as I have now. I wouldn't have known how to deal with this problem at that time.

- I'm grateful I discovered this difficulty in ample time to work to correct the problem before it can cause irreparable damage.

- I'm glad that, over the past few years, I've built relationships of trust and respect with many of my team members in our organization; I am confident that I can call on them for effort and advice in this challenging situation.

- I'm grateful that the creativity I use and the effort I expend in the process of overcoming this obstacle will demonstrate to my colleagues and followers that I am the kind of individual who can help them develop and use more of their own potential for achievement.

PAUL J. MEYER

Examining the list, you may be struck by the thought that every obstacle or difficulty really holds a benefit that you might miss if you do not work through the problem. Your list of similar reasons becomes objective evidence of personal gain. The exciting challenge before you is the task of finding the best way around, through, or over the obstacle or roadblock you've encountered.

Those who have never struggled with difficulty can never know the full joy of success. At any level of leadership, the real thrill of success comes from realizing that, by your own persistence and effort, you have averted or eluded failure.

Of course, you and your team members are completely free to choose how you will react to adversity. You can allow difficulty to defeat you, or you can see obstacles as opportunities to use more of your collective potential.

Truly great leaders adamantly reject the dire warnings of negative thinkers who point out the possibility of error, who offer continuing discouragement, or who doubt the potential and ability of effective leadership. They listen, instead, to their inner voice of confidence and determination. They create that inner voice by searching for ways to achieve their goals—and not for excuses to give up and quit.

Courage and Determination

Courage to Dream

Effective leaders understand that qualities like imagination, creativity, and potential for success become useful only when they are put to work to achieve a meaningful goal. An integral part of this actualization process involves learning to dream...to use imagination and creative power in ways that will produce specific directions and goals for themselves and their team members.

But it takes courage to dream. The moment any leader generates a unique and creative idea, he or she becomes a minority of one. The truly creative leader stands alone until others can be persuaded to join in pursuit of the dream. Even then, the leader continues to be the only individual who has a singular depth of belief and quality of commitment to the dream. Thus do leaders come to understand the loneliness that is born of singleness of purpose.

For a leader and team members alike, being alone is often a frightening experience. That's why all of us require courage to become dreamers.

For many team members, the ability to dream may have been almost completely destroyed by negative past experiences. During childhood, the process of conditioning robs many of us of the ability to dream. Teachers and parents alike may deliver stern admonitions to quit daydreaming and get to work; the child infers that any attempt to crystallize or visualize the future is somehow a wasted effort. Similarly, many of your team members may have acquired the belief that wanting anything—for any reason—is somehow selfish and wrong.

The sad consequence of these childhood experiences is the large percentage of adults who have largely lost their ability to dream. Before leaders and team members can reach the level of

155

success they desire and deserve, they must first rid themselves of the notion that dreaming and yearning is a manifestation of wasted effort or selfish greed.

But discarding these old beliefs, whether in a family environment or in the world of work, requires courage...courage to be different.

Nothing in the universe exists without a reason...hence, every potential talent and ability in you and your team members was placed in you for a specific purpose. Because leaders can dream, they *must*. And leaders also must bear the responsibility of sharing the necessity for dreaming with team members who may lack the courage to visualize greater achievement.

Team members should understand that their imagination and creativity—no matter how damaged or dormant—are intended to be used, not wasted. Members of your organization deserve to possess their dreams if they are willing to pursue them and work diligently to bring them into reality. Personal success is not reserved for the leadership elite; everyone deserves to enjoy it. But success begins with dreaming—and dreaming requires courage.

Courage to Face Yourself

Some leaders manage to find the courage to dream and imagine, but they lack the mental fortitude to face themselves. They fail to acknowledge their own weaknesses, to draw on their own strengths, and to analyze where they stand now in relation to where they want to go. This is a human trait; we all have elements of personality or personal habits with which we are not entirely pleased. Of course, it is tempting to deny that these personality characteristics or personal traits even exist, but such a course leads only to complacency. Without the courage to face yourself, all your dreams fade into meaningless fantasies…nothing will ever come of them.

As a leader, you should exercise the courage necessary to make a fair assessment of your own personal resources. This assessment should paint a realistic picture of where you stand now in relation to your own personal and professional journey. While you may not be entirely satisfied with what you learn about yourself, you cannot afford to feel discouraged.

The strengths and weaknesses you have developed at this point in your personal journey are completely unrelated to your worth as a human being or to your potential for highly effective leadership. Your assessment is information about past growth, not your future potential. Armed with this information, you can begin to build the final portion of your bridge across the leadership gap.

Many leaders have never given a great deal of thought to the process of self-knowledge and self-examination; the process may feel vaguely uncomfortable to them. Of course, new or unknown situations are always somewhat frightening. But self-knowledge is a tool that allows leaders and team members alike to take control of their future…to command their own destiny. As such, self-knowledge is a tool that must be used with courage.

Courage to Start

You are familiar with the basic law of physics that states that a body at rest tends to remain at rest. This law is responsible for a simple leadership fact—the quality most crucial to attaining success for yourself and your organization is the courage to begin!

It requires more energy or power to start a car or to take off in an airplane than it does to just keep going. More force is required to change direction than to proceed in a straight line. This law works in your organization as well. If you and your team members are sitting back and waiting for your proverbial ship to come in, you'll find it incredibly easy to keep on sitting there! Circumstances will never drop dreams into your lap. The longer you sit back and wait, the more dynamite will be required to blast you and your organization into productive action.

> Courage is required to choose a challenging goal and begin to move toward it. Once you and your team members have developed the courage required to begin moving toward your dreams, sheer momentum will help you keep moving. Actually, overcoming inertia requires the greatest amount of energy and courage. Once you and your organization are in motion, another law of physics works in your favor: A body in motion tends to stay in motion.

> RANDY SLECHTA

Courage to Risk

Without risks, no leader can become truly great. Why? Because no real progress can be achieved, no new product created, and no new innovations championed. All require some degree of risk...and without courage, leaders take no risks.

The feeling of security is a basic human need. In their broadest sense, security and safety can be threatened by almost any departure from the present norm. If your dream is to introduce a new product line, for example, risks to your security are somewhat obvious. While you will probably not be in any physical danger, there is the danger that the new product line might not be successful. Loss of income and investment capital could create financial difficulties for your organization. Your friends and colleagues might call you foolhardy. Your banker might even refuse to back you with needed financial resources.

Certainly, reaching for the stars is a risky business. But your failure to take those risks sets up an even more dangerous risk— the possibility that you and your team will miss the chance to fulfill dreams, to develop potential and ability, and to achieve goals that best express fulfillment of your purpose.

The Source of Leadership Courage

How you respond to the challenges and decisions you face is not just a matter of your personal choice; it is the defining moment of your leadership experience. Any leader can retreat in fear; only the most effective leaders can instinctively push forward with courage, conviction, and determination.

The choice is yours to make. This is not to say that the choice is easy. For the effective leader, the courage to make the choice comes from deep within. Leaders who possess courage also possess the qualities necessary to help themselves and their team members become more than they are.

Among leaders, no choice is more difficult than deciding to act with courage and conviction. But once leaders push themselves to act courageously in a single area of life or in one aspect of their business role, it becomes progressively easier to act with courage in other areas and in other situations.

No commodity is more rare—or more highly prized— than iron-willed commitment to a cause or crusade.

Unfortunately, leaders must realize that no one can have courage for them. Effective leaders consciously choose courage as an option. As a leader, you open up new pathways to your objectives when you choose to act with courage. You discover new depths of resources and potential within yourself and your team members. Perhaps for the first time in your leadership career, you realize that you and your colleagues really *can* take charge of your lives and that you can do with them what you will.

Determination and Personal Responsibility

The Buck Stops Here!

The sign on President Harry Truman's desk reminded everyone who saw it that Truman bore the weight of important decisions. Today, virtually every leader shoulders some element of responsibility for outcomes. The burden you bear may not be as great as was Truman's—and you may not communicate it as bluntly as he did—but the same sentiment still applies. As a leader, you are often the responsible party. For initiatives you design or approve, for policies and procedures you develop or implement, and for projects you oversee or champion, the buck stops with you.

To reap the benefits that are inherently yours in life, you must accept personal responsibility for your actions. This is the only way you and your followers alike can begin to lay claim to the abundance of potential that is your birthright.

Accept the fact that nothing—absolutely *nothing*—you do in your organization will produce the successful results you desire until you as a leader choose to accept personal responsibility for what happens to you and your colleagues.

The Blame Game

Unfortunately, many people are accustomed to blaming others for their own shortcomings. Children blame their parents. Students blame the teachers. Employees blame the employer. Criminals blame society or their victims. And all of us, at one time or another, blame the government!

> When we expend energy and time blaming others for our own failures and for who we are as individuals, there's less energy left for growth, improvement, and success. Blaming others, reliving past failures, and repeating mistakes are merely ways leaders and followers alike have devised to avoid accepting personal responsibility for their actions.
>
> REX HOUZE

Leaders who have made the decision to accept personal responsibility for who they are recognize that their own knowledge of past mistakes and failures, their own admission of personality faults and negative habit patterns, and their own understanding of the powerful negative conditioning that has brought them to this point are all merely items of information. All these things combine to tell effective leaders where to start on the road to achieving the true success of which they are capable.

Indeed, the failures of the past are significant only if you repeat them or refuse to learn from them. Although parents, teachers, and society in general may truly deserve some of the credit or blame for who you are today, you alone are responsible for what you can become.

Not only must you, as a leader, accept personal responsibility for who you are, you also must accept personal responsibility for your feelings and emotions as well.

If you find yourself feeling afraid, feeling hesitant, or feeling discouraged, recognize that no one but you is responsible for the fact that you are experiencing a negative emotion.

The simple fact is that no one else and no outside circumstance can make you feel any particular way. Your team members and events can certainly contribute to situations that create various emotions, but how you feel about those situations is, in the final analysis, your own personal choice. When leaders refuse to let the actions and words of others affect their attitude, they exhibit the kind of maturity that allows them to take charge of their own lives...and this same maturity goes a long way toward convincing team members and colleagues that their leader truly holds their best interests close to heart.

Accepting Responsibility for Leadership Actions

Once you accept personal responsibility for who you are and how you feel, the next logical step is the acceptance of personal responsibility for the actions you take. When leaders accept personal responsibility for their actions, they avoid comparing themselves to others. They evaluate their own actions against a standard—the standard of personal and organizational goals that will measure their own excellence.

Leaders who accept personal responsibility for their own actions don't judge their performance by a clock. They don't quit for the day just because they have fulfilled the minimum daily requirements for keeping the doors open. Armed with personal responsibility, effective leaders go the extra mile to keep their commitments to themselves, to their team members, and to their customers as well.

You may have noticed that highly effective leaders often exceed the best that others expect of them. This is because these individuals have made a habit of rising to meet needs as they become aware of them. They understand that the one leadership factor with the largest potential for outstanding success is their willingness to take personal responsibility for the organization they lead.

The Benefits of Personal Responsibility

In the area of personal and organizational growth, you have a magnificent opportunity to seize personal responsibility and exercise it for greater good. As an effective leader, you can experience unusual personal growth both as an individual and as a businessperson.

And, in a very real sense, you become a merchant of personal growth and success for those with whom you work. The product you are selling is the same product you've used yourself—the personal habits and behavior characteristics that lead to the achievement of individual and organizational dreams. Because you have become a product of that product—through dreaming great dreams, making noble plans, and daily pursuing them—those around you will be able to sense your personal growth and want to experience the same thing in their own lives.

But personal and professional growth is your responsibility. Just as you cannot force team members to become more than they are, no one can force you to grow. No one else can accept the responsibility of growing in your place. The question you must answer is an important one: Are you willing to pay the price to accept the responsibility for personal growth?

Think well on your answer. Your iron-willed determination to succeed hinges upon your decision to accept personal responsibility for your own personal development. The trust that you place in others will be strengthened or shattered by your decision to grow personally or to stay the way you are. The desire to achieve new and significant goals will be dramatically increased or reduced to nil, depending on your decision. The dreams you've dreamed and the plans you've made all rely on accepting personal responsibility for progress, growth, and change.

While the result of accepting personal responsibility is the true freedom to become what your Creator destined you to be, the real benefit is the success you vividly imagine, ardently desire, sincerely believe, and enthusiastically act upon.

What Happens without Responsibility?

Other leaders have refused to accept personal responsibility and have fallen into apathy and bondage. This fate must not befall you.

Other leaders have rejected personal responsibility and have failed miserably. Their failure must not become yours.

Other leaders have feared personal responsibility and have thus allowed incredible opportunities to slip through their grasp. Their loss must not be your loss.

Other leaders have neglected to accept personal responsibility and have drifted into the depths of mediocrity. Their waste of potential and ability must be theirs alone!

The acceptance of personal responsibility is a creed—a way of living that will help bridge the leadership gap. For the next millennium, it stands as an ideal for your organization, for our nation, for whole societies, and for the entire planet. Why? Because when free people—leaders and team members alike—dare to accept personal responsibility for themselves and their own lives, they bring incredible freedom for achievement to the organizations to which they contribute. One person at a time, they bring freedom to the entire human race.

Leaders must accept personal responsibility for their own success and failure. I look upon every failure as a learning experience. During my lifetime, I have started or invested in more than a hundred businesses. Only 35 percent have succeeded—the rest failed. But by taking an appropriate risk, I have expanded my own capabilities. This, too, is a freedom—the freedom to develop and use my full potential for success. I believe that this is the kind of freedom worth having—the freedom of leaders and followers alike to reach within themselves, to find the potential placed there by their Creator and use that potential to grow and to achieve and to fulfill the purpose for which they were created.

PAUL J. MEYER

9

The Bridge to Change

Leadership at the Crossroads

Change as Opportunity

Progress, growth, and change are the order of humanity. Truly great leaders embrace change with open arms because they know and understand that without change, nothing survives.

Change is an integral part of life, of course. Change is an essential element in the challenge of leadership. After all, if nothing ever changed, leadership would be a simple process of putting working procedures into place and watching them operate. But because change is inevitable, leadership is largely the challenge of managing it.

"Negative capability" is a term coined by poet John Keats. He defined it as the capability to withstand uncertainties, mysteries, doubts, without irritable reaching after fact or reason. I like to think of negative capability as the ability to bounce back from failure, to overcome obstacles, to take a calculated risk. You waste not a second in doubt, frustration, or wondering why you're facing obstacles. Obstacles are a fact of life...negative capability is a measure of your ability to focus on positive possibilities for overcoming them. Singapore businessman Y. Y. Wong put it best: Negative capability allows you to refuse to let the negative forces in your environment control you and your emotions.

PAUL J. MEYER

Different leaders and team members offer differing reactions to change. Some become frightened, depressed, or even paralyzed...incapable of taking action of any kind. Others see change as the challenge it is—they are inspired, energized, and revitalized. Leaders can no more prevent or avoid change than they can single-handedly stop the ocean tides. Change roars along like a mighty river...but it is a river that can be properly channeled and utilized as a driving force for achievement.

Three Keys to Constructive Change

How do effective leaders learn to view change as an opportunity to learn and grow? Quite simply, they build on the five pillars of the leadership bridge. They work to crystallize their thinking, help team members develop all six areas of life, and involve those individuals in the process of anticipating, tracking, and redefining the course of change.

To deal constructively with any kind of change, leaders must possess clearly defined organizational goals. For leaders and team members alike, change is often something to be feared because the consequences of change are largely unknown. Achievement in the midst of chaotic, unfamiliar, and changing circumstances is a much more work-intensive process than achievement in ordinary surroundings. A clearly defined program of organizational goals serves to make change less daunting, less threatening, and more manageable because the goals define the changes.

In most cases, of course, the changes seem to define the goals. Change itself is often the master of the organization. It tends to set the course and manage the team effort toward a destination of its own choosing. Possessed of a clearly defined organizational plan of action, highly effective leaders are able to turn the tables on change. The goals define the changes to be made, the direction or course to be followed, and the contribution of each team member to make certain those goals are achieved successfully.

Additionally, organizational goals tend to alleviate fear of change. If for no other reason, this should recommend clearly defined goals to every leader and manager! Organizational goals serve to spell out in detail the benefits that leaders and team members will enjoy as a result of change. And, they help each member of the organization construct a clear mental image of the rewarding conditions that will be established as a result of change.

Consider the second key to constructive change: encouraging the personal growth of team members. We've already made the point that personal growth and Total Person status are not reserved for some sort of leadership elite. Leaders who involve their team members in a planned process of personal growth actually hasten the process of achieving organizational goals. Team members quickly discover that the easiest path to achieving their own personal goals lies in helping the organization reach its goals.

It's our belief that individuals seldom leave organizations for better pay or better working conditions. Instead, they leave most often because they are dissatisfied with their own personal growth. When team members grow personally and become more well-rounded individuals, they generate their own supply of positive attitudes, enthusiasm, and excitement. All three habits of thought are essential elements in any effort to deal constructively with change.

Why? Because team members who tend to support themselves through these enabling attitudes also tend to support the organization...and their leaders and other team members as well. Simply stated, the team member who is growing personally finds renewed excitement in the work...and that excitement is contagious!

Team members who are "green and growing" develop mental attitudes and work habits that are conducive to change. Team members who are "ripe and rotting," on the other hand, resist change and cling to old, unproductive attitudes and habits. The leader's choice is simple: Empower these individuals with the opportunity to grow and develop in every area of life, or allow them to waste their potential for happiness and achievement. Leaders who consign their team members to the ranks of the forgotten are always frighteningly susceptible to the destructive effects of negative, unharnessed change.

> When our children don't get positive attention, they sometimes resort to negative behavior to attract the attention they desire. The same is true in an organization—without positive attention, team members can begin to create negative changes to get the attention and recognition they need. Giving team members challenging assignments and adequate rewards will keep them "green and growing" and keep them focused on the organization's short-range and long-range goals.
>
> RANDY SLECHTA

Third, leaders who effectively manage change strive to involve team members in the process of planning, tracking, and evaluating new circumstances, new situations, and new procedures. While ordinary leaders develop some kind of "oversight committee" composed of a few team members who are expected to give tacit approval to the process of change, highly effective leaders involve every member of the team. Each individual, after all, has something unique to offer—a different perspective, a different idea, or a different attitude. Great leaders see this uniqueness as a treasure chest and strive to make it an integral element of the process of managing change.

Team member participation gives the individual members of your organization a sense of ownership. This vicarious ownership serves to encourage a deeper commitment to the overall success of any organization. Indeed, team member contributions engender loyalty, involvement, and personal commitment that bond team members to the organization for the long term. Vicarious ownership helps reduce the implicit threat of change because it works to make available every team member's intimate knowledge of organizational problems and potential.

A Safety Net?

The best leaders are always fully aware that team members may not always be as certain of the outcome of change as are the leaders themselves. That's why, when asking their people to change, they are careful to provide some sort of safety net.

A safety net, while it can take many forms, serves only one purpose: It is a provision for handling unexpected obstacles, roadblocks, and other adversities. The provisions of any safety net are based on positive support, including specific feedback, extraordinarily open and more frequent communication, and the increased visibility and involvement of the leaders themselves.

Of course, team members strive for security—they want to

know that they will be able to fulfill their own needs and the needs of their families. No safety net provides that kind of iron-clad assurance; the value of a safety net is largely mental rather than financial. Confronted with change and crisis, many leaders retreat into obscurity and silence. They pretend that problems do not exist, even though most members of the organization can see the symptoms develop. As a result, team members become nervous and uneasy...hardly healthy habits of thought for maximum productivity. In contrast, team members are reassured and will frequently redouble their efforts when they feel that leaders are making an honest effort to communicate challenges and are putting forth the time and effort required to stem the tide of negative change.

Confronting Problems and Difficulties

Highly effective leaders plan to handle change-related problems. There are, of course, some specific action tools leaders can use in the face of change-induced challenges and difficulties.

It goes almost without saying that a comprehensive goals program will do more to anticipate roadblocks and problems than any other tool. This is because an integral element of such a plan involves the design of a pathway around the problems and hardships that are likely to develop. This goals program can become a catalyst for carefully created procedures that effectively handle problems before they can cause damage to the organization.

Some leaders choose to avoid this sort of pre-problem planning, opting instead to allow any problems that arise to take care of themselves. This is a huge mistake...and a deadly trap. Effective leaders avoid procrastinating in problem situations, and they communicate with their team members in an effort to encourage the participation of others and to take advantage of their combined creativity.

As a leader, you may already realize that while you can choose to embrace some change, some change also will be thrust upon you. In either case, you will find that you are able to successfully manage change by making workable plans, implementing your designs, and carefully monitoring progress.

> Over the past twenty-five years, I've used a couple of simple exercises to show why people resist change. I have participants clasp their hands and then ask them if they are comfortable...and why. Then I have them change the way their fingers are interlocked. Asked to choose between this "new" clasp and the "old" way, they invariably pick the old way. I also ask them to fold their arms across their chest and note how their arms are positioned. When they are asked to cross their arms a different way, most people look like a windmill! People resist change for two reasons: It is usually uncomfortable, and it threatens their status quo. When leaders ask their team members to change, they need to keep in mind that the natural tendency is exactly the opposite!
>
> REX HOUZE

When the space shuttle leaves Earth, great concern focuses on the spacecraft as it builds up maximum aerodynamic pressure just seconds after launch. Effective leaders demonstrate their greatest concern and management efforts as their organization passes through the area of maximum change. By carefully monitoring progress and growth, the pressure of change is reduced to a measurable, manageable quality.

The Option of Restructuring

The last few years have seen organizational restructuring emerge as a quick fix for change-induced problems. And it is true that restructuring is a viable method of dealing with the effects of change. Restructuring can be carried out on several different levels—leaders can restructure the entire organization or just revamp the assignment of responsibilities. Either way, effective restructuring is no quick fix.

To make restructuring acceptable to team members, leaders must begin by making careful plans. Those plans first involve the organization's goals program. Leaders who lack clearly defined organizational goals usually use restructuring as a stop-gap measure, hoping to delay the inexorable march of change long enough to find something that will permanently stem the tide.

Leaders who have involved their team members in the development of organizational goals are often surprised to find that other individuals recognize the need for restructuring first! Defensive or inflexible attitudes and habits are discarded when team members become an integral part of the goal-setting process; they typically view restructuring as a positive, productive necessity...another step toward the achievement of the organization's ultimate goals. When team members are involved in the process of setting goals, they are also involved in the process of goals achievement. If restructuring aids in that effort, team members will see it as a positive way of moving farther down the road to success.

Changes in the structure of an organization should be made gradually. Why? Because leaders and team members alike find smaller changes easier to assimilate and adjust to than larger changes. However, if the organization's goals program makes a full reorganization an absolute necessity, carrying out the complete restructuring all at once may be preferable to dragging it out. Dragged out long enough, restructuring can result in a serious loss of organizational stability...to say nothing of the loss of your own stability in the process!

Whatever time schedule you choose for your restructuring effort, be sure to involve team members in the planning process. Your key people deserve your reassurance and support; after all, they support and reassure the entire organization. When you present restructuring as growth-oriented change—as an opportunity for improvement—you will find that team members respond with increased productivity, better quality and service, and with a new awareness of their opportunity to contribute to both personal and organizational success.

The Secret of Surviving Change

In the final analysis, surviving crisis and change demands one quality of every leader—flexibility. Flexibility is the ability to bend without breaking. It gives you the ability to hold fast to your goals, your mission, and your cause. Flexibility gives you the ability to separate the means from the end result. Inflexible leaders lack that delicate balance between maintaining control of the organization and striving to fulfill the needs of team members. Flexible leaders, on the other hand, are keenly sensitive to the needs of the individuals within the organization. They are willing to make minor adjustments in their plan of action to accommodate those needs.

That willingness to make minor adjustments fosters respect among team members. When you are willing to cater to their needs, they willingly follow you and your leadership. Thus, team members become the effective harbingers of change; you can depend on them to respond positively as they play their part in the effort to keep the organization on track. Their efforts are conducive to organizational stability—and your flexibility has created their willingness to go the extra mile.

In every arena of life—in families, schools, civic organizations, and businesses—flexibility is the key to positive and productive change. Flexibility, more than perhaps any other characteristic of highly effective leaders, constructively blends both personal and organizational goals. The end result is committed individuals...team members who are sold out to the achievement of your objectives as well as their own.

What Comes First?

Managing Priorities Effectively

In times of unrelenting change and challenge, leaders and managers are continually faced with the need to determine priorities. This is another area in which a working goals program makes a valuable contribution. Such a program of organizational objectives helps every member of the team identify what comes first, what comes second, and so on.

The action steps for achieving specific organizational goals determine which part of the effort will be yours and what work will be given to other members of your team. I believe that the most effective way of choosing your own activities involves determining their time cost. Based on your annual income and the number of hours you work per week, it is possible to determine with a fair degree of accuracy what you are being paid for each week, each day, and each hour on the job. When you realize what your time is actually worth in terms of dollars and cents, it becomes far easier to choose the items you will perform personally and those you will delegate to others in the organization.

Comparing the cost of your time with the worth of the activity involved is an effective way to set both personal and organizational priorities. You should not squander a good deal of your valuable time on projects that can be handled by those whose time costs your organization less money.

Some leaders choose to establish priorities by evaluating the contribution each specific activity will make to the achievement of the team's overall goals. Obviously, activities that help move you and your organization closer to predetermined objectives demand a higher priority than those that will produce little real benefit. Any leader's time is best spent on items that produce the highest rate of financial return for the organization. If time is left over, it can be applied to activities that are lower in priority.

The Value of an Hour

When you know the dollar value of each hour of your working time, you can couple that figure with the value of the activity itself and the contribution the activity will make to overall organizational goals. You should also have a good idea of the amount of time the activity will consume. Then you are ready to choose a particular strategy for handling that activity...or to decide whether it should be handled at all!

Some activities, of course, are essential to the smooth operation of the organization. Yet the level of skill required to accomplish them is often so low that you should not spend your time on that activity. Instead, find someone on your team to whom you can delegate the activity. If that individual's time costs your company less than your own time, you've just made an additional profit.

Moreover, you have helped a member of your team grow and improve. As if that weren't enough benefit, delegation goes a long way toward establishing clear priorities and values for the balance of the team as well.

Effective leaders have learned to delegate low-cost items, routine activities, and anything that can be done by someone else without personal attention and intervention on the part of the leader.

Many leaders fail to develop a clear understanding of priorities because they have failed to create adequate job descriptions for other members of the team. In this case, team members have little or no idea of what they should be doing with their time. The notion of establishing priorities for themselves and other people is typically an exercise in abstract thinking. Full job descriptions, on the other hand, give leaders a clear picture of the workflow and how assignments are handled.

Effective leaders look for items of work that can be rearranged quickly and efficiently. These are typically items that are related to each other and tasks that might be done more quickly and easily by one person than by several team members. It is, of course, the leader's responsibility to make certain that each job or task is actually completed by the team member who can do it most quickly and most accurately.

Priorities help leaders spot those items or activities that should be eliminated altogether. These are items that provide so little contribution to overall organizational goals that the time to perform them is not a justifiable expense. The best leaders are often those who are willing—even eager in some cases—to do away with reports, activities, and rituals that have managed to survive long enough to outlive their usefulness.

Keeping in Touch with the Changing Organization

Staying Informed

Along with planning ahead and establishing priorities, staying informed is a critical attribute for effective leaders who embrace organizational change. While tedious and time-consuming to establish, a system for handling each part of the day-to-day routine cuts down on the number of decisions that must be made by leaders and managers. Additionally, a system helps transform problems into automatic procedures and ensures that the individual most qualified will handle a given situation when it arises.

Effective leaders eliminate a great deal of the anxiety that typically accompanies change when they already have three key elements in place:

- *Clearly defined procedures* should govern all routine functions within the organization. This is where an up-to-date procedures manual comes into play; such a manual helps to train new team members and to keep everyone tracking toward completion of a specified activity. Additionally, clearly defined procedures help reduce time that might otherwise be used in giving instructions. They also help eliminate repetitive decision-making and prevent the accidental omission of important activities.

- *Regular reports* should be requested on a monthly basis—if not more frequently—from each team member in a position of leadership or management. The report should deal with items that are clearly linked to the achievement of specific organizational goals. To help team members engage in the planning process at their level, monthly reports should focus on accomplishments during the previous month, current serious problems and plans for solving them, and detailed plans for accomplishment in the month ahead.

- *Availability and accessibility* are two hallmarks of great leaders. Seldom do highly effective leaders lead on an absentee basis. They know that they must be available and accessible to provide direction, coaching, and encouragement to each member of the organization. A leader's accessibility has a profound effect on the attitude of the organization. Your accessibility—both physical and emotional—provides team members with the confidence to move forward.

- *Observation* is the talent most often employed by great leaders. These individuals have worked hard to become a good listener and a keen observer of people and events. They have learned to relate what they have observed to the organization's overall goals. Additionally, their skill enables them to pick up hints of trouble before some serious difficulty actually develops.

Through the habit of observation, effective leaders arm themselves with the tools necessary to eliminate problems before they can pose a serious threat to the aims of the organization. All successful leaders strive to stay informed and abreast of change within their organization. In this way, they are equipped to respond effectively to the challenge of change and to act creatively to implement solutions that will improve the productivity of the entire team.

The Stress of Change

Can Stress Work FOR You?

The stressless leader is a perpetuated myth. The fact is that every leader and manager, in any facet of any organization, experiences some level of stress. The most effective leaders, however, develop their skills for using stress as a force for achievement rather than a destructive entity.

When does stress strike most leaders? Typically, stress occurs when conditions produce an awareness that some action is needed to solve a problem, satisfy a particular need, or prevent some negative result. When leaders believe that the pressure to act can be met by calculated and well-defined action, stress is a constructive agent. But if the perceived need requires more time, greater skill, or more money, stress can become a destructive force.

Indeed, executive stress can pack the same dynamic force as organizational change. Often, the only real difference is that fewer individuals are affected by stress, and the time span in which problems must be solved grows correspondingly smaller as well.

Manifestations of Stress

Stress manifests itself both physically and psychologically...and sometimes in both ways. Primitive emotions, activated and encouraged by stress, cause leaders and followers alike to rise up to meet a perceived threat. Body functions speed up; the muscles are stimulated and prepared for extraordinary effort. If some sort of strenuous physical activity follows this physical preparation, the body returns to normal just as soon as the need has been met or the threat has been vanquished.

If, however, the perceived threat isn't eliminated by the body's activity, the physical preparation continues...and continues...and continues. The body keeps on preparing itself to meet a threat. Often exhaustion sets in before the threat manifests itself.

Dealing with stress isn't an easy task for many leaders. They take antacids to ease stomach discomfort and swallow painkillers to alleviate back pain. And these are just the beginning; all sorts of physical ailments plague individuals who live in a constant state of stress.

The psychological effects are even more damaging. Short tempers and frayed nerves are the outward manifestations of chronic stress that refuses to be satisfied by a reasonable amount of activity. But the greatest damage is done within, to attitude and spirit. Unremitting stress destroys the thrill and excitement of achievement because no result seems good enough. Continual stress robs work of its pure joy.

The toll continues to mount. Stress-induced dissatisfaction with personal activity and individual productivity leads to a breakdown in relationships between people at home and at work. Undue stress hampers decision-making effectiveness, decreases individual productivity, and blocks mental creativity.

Stress and Change

Stress is often a manifestation of change, and change is often a result of stress. Both are opportunities and positive challenges; neither enjoys great popularity. But without stress, motivation withers and dies. Stress and change are essential elements in the order of life.

Effective leaders handle stress in much the same way that they handle change—they look for the positive aspects rather than dwell on the negative effects. Stress is a challenge to any leader's creativity. It is a welcome opportunity to showcase leadership performance. Great leaders understand this opportunity and seize it. Winston Churchill's talk of "blood, tears, toil, and sweat" was the rallying cry for Britain in the darkest days of World War II.

Why would stress-induced metaphors serve to motivate you and your team members? Simply stated, your language and behavior reflect your attitude that stress is a challenge and an opportunity. Used in this positive way, stress and change inspire people in every organization to act, to achieve, and to dig deep for the best within themselves.

Change and Leadership Burnout

What Is Burnout?

Many business leaders talk about burnout as if it were a living, breathing thing. Actually, burnout is a *condition* brought about by unrelieved work stress and results in a high degree of emotional exhaustion. Of course, personal productivity is dramatically decreased as well.

The best leaders understand that preventing burnout among team members is just as vital a concern as preventing burnout within themselves. Indeed, leaders become critical role models as they demonstrate the way in which they constructively manage change and stress to prevent burnout in their own lives.

Effective leaders strive to identify specific causes of stress; then they plan and carry out equally specific actions to minimize or eliminate the causes altogether. Common causes of burnout inducing stress might include work overload, excessive demands on time, unrealistic expectations, and interpersonal conflicts.

Leaders who involve their team members in goal-setting exercises for their particular positions find that the levels of uncertainty and conflict are considerably reduced. Uncertainty fades away in the presence of a plan of action and clearly defined goals; role conflicts decline when team members have a clear definition of their own responsibilities. Additionally, team member input helps leaders and followers alike develop strategies for handling stress and change in day-to-day work activity.

The best way to handle burnout is to prevent it from happening altogether.

Effective leaders show their team members an attitude of genuine caring and concern. This eliminates one of the major

183

sources of stress within the organization. Team members receive strong emotional support from leaders who pay attention to their concerns and problems. Successful leaders are always engaged in information gathering conversations that will provide them with the information necessary to cope with pressure, change, and performance expectations.

Effective leaders know that the more control team members exert over their own lives, the more likely they are to meet the goals for organizational productivity. When team members are achieving their own personal goals, they are far more inclined to put forth the effort necessary to achieve company goals as well. Let stress and change inspire you to become more sensitive to the needs of your team members. While you inspire other members of the organization to remain productive and to achieve specific performance goals, you become more skillful in managing stress, change, and preventing burnout.

Change and the Balancing Act

Keeping Your Perspective

Why are you doing what you're doing? The same question screams at us again. This time it howls alongside the winds of change. Presumably, effective leaders and team members alike develop plans of action in all six areas of life for the express purpose of reducing stress, planning for change, eliminating old habits and attitudes, and enhancing their enjoyment of life.

But when the gale force of change buffets you from pillar to pillar on the leadership bridge, you will find yourself asking this same question again and again and again. The answer is in six parts—one for each area of your own life. In the quest to manage change, you cannot forget to continue working to change yourself.

In the *financial and career* aspect of your own life, strive to exercise the same careful watch over your personal finances as you do for your organization. Don't lose sight of your career goals; they are guideposts that you can cling to for support when the blizzards of change assail you. This area of life is critical to your continued success. It provides you with the income, the influence, and the sense of accomplishment that helps you achieve goals in the other five areas.

In terms of your personal *physical and health* area, you can weaken the effects of stress and change by adding a sensible diet, a good exercise program, and adequate rest. Your body is the support structure for your active and creative mind.

In the *family and home* aspect of life, you can apply some of the time and energy you've saved through crystallized thinking and specific goals management at work. Strive to maintain worthwhile relationships with every member of your family. You will find it easy to demonstrate the same care and concern for them as you have for your team members.

The *mental and educational* area offers you continued opportunities to grow in knowledge of your career field and other areas of interest. Stimulate yourself to think and ponder important ideas by making a point of reading something new each day.

The *spiritual and ethical* area of your life also demands attention. Work to become the kind of person you want to be—someone who supports the values you want to demonstrate to others. You have an opportunity to give back to others some of the blessings and rewards that have been given to you...don't fail to do just that!

Many leaders find that the *social and cultural* relationships they develop in that area of life extend no farther than the company doors. Invoke change to help yourself develop a wider circle of friends with whom you share mutual interests.

The Dynamics of Growth

While you may be assaulted and confronted by the forces of change and stress on a daily basis, you cannot afford to neglect your own personal and professional growth. By now, you've grasped the important dynamics of that growth...the same dynamics that apply to growth within your team members and within your organization.

The dynamic of growth is *change*.

If you fail to change, you fail to grow. If you fail to help your team members change, they fail to grow. If you and your team members fail to move forward through change, your organization doesn't just remain stagnant—it begins a downward spiral toward oblivion.

> *Search for a cause greater than yourself, some worthwhile endeavor that you can support with your time, effort, and money.*

For yourself and your organization, the process of planning growth takes on paramount importance. The old saying, "Fail to plan, plan to fail," is literally true. The key to managing personal and organizational change lies in the acquired ability to crystallize and clearly define the future. Leaders who possess and utilize this ability bridge the leadership gap by moving across the five pillars to the higher ground of greater accomplishment.

10

Crossing the Leadership Bridge

Developing Human Potential

The Power of Effective Leadership

Great leaders take on many roles; chief among them is developer of human potential.

Each individual on your team has the capacity to benefit from your efforts to help them develop personally and professionally. Within each person lies the potential to become far more than they are. That expectation—the development of human potential for success and achievement—is best realized through effective leadership.

As you strive to bridge the leadership gap, you may develop a deeper appreciation for this responsibility. After all, no one really has more power than you to influence team members and to directly affect their level of productivity. The responsibility becomes even more weighty when you realize that, to your team members, you *are* the organization they serve.

Why do team members typically possess this singularly narrow view? Because while you may or may not run the entire organization, you do at least run their part of it. You encounter daily opportunities to make decisions, determine schedules, recommend or offer promotions and raises, establish or alter procedures, and provide your team members with other news and information—good and bad.

Middle managers wear yet another hat. They represent their portion of the work force to upper management. This forces a unique dichotomy; to do their job with confidence, middle managers must have the confidence, respect, and trust of both sides of the organization...the rank-and-file and upper management.

Leaders who run the organization, on the other hand, find that success is nothing so much as a balancing act. They are required to balance the potential and desire of the work force against the typically ponderous requirements of the business.

Wherever you may find yourself, the leadership spectrum exerts unique and unrelenting demands. You'll find that a continuing program of training and personal development is a key to securing the confidence and trust of your team members...and to ensuring the overall success of the organization. All training has but one goal: to develop a more productive and more versatile work force. Training helps team members gain greater satisfaction from the work they do. They take more pride in their product, their equipment, and the organization as a whole.

Personal development, on the other hand, inspires team members to take greater pride in themselves and in their potential for achievement. While personal development often manifests itself in intangible ways—like an enhanced spirit of cooperation and a greater sense of pride—it creates valuable benefits when coupled with training. The result of training and personal development is a combined reduction in costs and an increase in quality, productivity, and overall performance.

The point is that training and personal development typically produce few benefits when applied independently. Workers may gain greater satisfaction from the work they do. But if they are still dissatisfied with themselves, the work will continue to suffer. Conversely, workers may feel excited about who they are and where they are going in life, but without specific skill building and job related training, they may become frustrated at their inability to climb the ladder to greater success.

The Crucible of Team Development

Our team members are often asked what one attitude leaders and managers should change to enhance overall effectiveness. They always reply that leaders and managers should give up the notion that training and personal development are luxuries. Effective leaders who are genuinely concerned with team member efficiency, productivity, and happiness, realize that training and personal development are absolute necessities.

Some leaders, of course, work to avoid training team members because they fear that eventually a team member will replace them at the helm of the organization. You should choose to look on this possibility as an incredible benefit. If you have no one prepared to take your place, you are destined to stay just where you are! Some managers avoid training because they believe the trainees will advance past them. This happens in every organization. In our international companies, for example, Randy Slechta was trained by Joe Baxter. Now Randy runs the organization. At LMI, Rex Houze was a distributor who was coached by a home office manager; now Rex is president of the company.

Leaders and managers who feel plagued by insecurity and fear of training should remember that they have not yet reached the ultimate limit for earnings and advancement.

> There are always ways to expand individual contribution to an organization...sometimes they require patient searching to uncover, but they are always there. There is no real reason for a leader or manager to expect that the organizational ladder offers no higher rung to climb.
>
> REX HOUZE

Many leaders and managers believe themselves too busy to take time to train and develop their team members...or themselves! The truth is that training yourself and your organization is an ongoing responsibility...it never ends. It stands to reason that the busier you are, the more important it is to gain new skills yourself and impart them to your team members. The freedom to do your job better carries a price tag: The cost is measured in effective training and development of your team members.

> If you want to move up the organizational ladder, develop others to take your place. Your job is not to perpetuate the status quo; your job is to teach, coach and encourage team members to develop their innate potential for greater achievement.
>
> RANDY SLECHTA

The Leader as Role Model

You will find that the attitudes of your team members toward training and performance improvement mirror...your own attitudes. How do you feel about innovation? About change? About improvement? How do you communicate your own estimate of their potential and the value of the work they do?

In the final analysis, your own attitudes establish the prevailing atmosphere of thought for your team members. Your own habits of thought determine how receptive team members will be to the pursuit of excellence. Your own commitment to personal and professional development determines how seriously team members approach both individual and on-the-job improvement.

Managing your attitudes toward your team members and personal growth is the litmus test of effective leadership. If you are successful, you reap rewards in three areas:

- *Improved Productivity:* Productivity improves because people improve; when they feel better about themselves and the job they are doing, team members follow the natural order of progress and growth just like everyone else.

- *Enhanced Interpersonal Relationships:* Team members are flesh and blood, just like you. As your workers continue to grow and improve, you develop a keen personal interest in their progress. The result is a closer relationship than ever before; your co-workers become your colleagues and, ultimately, your friends.

- *Better Morale, Better Attitudes:* When team members are growing personally and feeling better about themselves, the morale of the organization improves by the process of osmosis. One individual's positive attitude literally infects another...and so on. The dull, uncaring attitude that may have characterized your team members is quickly replaced by a positive, vibrant view of the organization and the contribution it makes to society.

Attracting and Keeping Your Team

The Law of Attraction

People join your team and become members of your organization when both promise to meet their basic individual needs. As long as that promise is kept, team members tend to stay. If the promise is somehow broken or ignored, they may leave in a hurry!

In finding and keeping team members who are committed to excellence, leaders should make the law of attraction come alive. A dynamic organization attracts dynamic team members. A work environment that stimulates creativity and makes the work experience a reward instead of a chore typically attracts individuals who are seeking the opportunity to contribute and to grow personally.

Of course, the organization's climate hinges on the attitudes, examples, and goals of the leader. The best leaders carefully design and nurture an atmosphere of positive attitudes, trust, and cooperation. This atmosphere, in turn, nurtures continuous individual improvement and productivity. In a word, such an atmosphere makes creativity and success acceptable.

The foundation of this successful climate is composed of clear expectations. Crystallized thinking and well-laid plans provide a strong and steady platform upon which to build organizational climate. But clear expectations also must form integral parts of the structure. Indeed, they become the walls within which the positive and growth-oriented climate is created.

How? Take job descriptions, for example. Well-written job descriptions serve to outline responsibilities, authority for decision-making and other expected activity. Team members, however, should be encouraged to participate in defining their own jobs. They should not just be handed a featureless job description and told to follow it.

Why? Because no two people ever function the same way, even when placed in exactly the same position. New team members should be allowed the creative freedom to shape and define their job to fit their individual talents and abilities. Leaders may even want to reconstruct different aspects of the organization so that, over time, the strengths and interests of all team members are fully utilized. These kinds of changes are the harbingers of growth and advancement—and they typically increase productivity as well.

Effective leaders work to supplement sterile job descriptions with one-on-one discussions which give team members an opportunity to ask questions, offer suggestions, and negotiate adjustments that would help them be more productive. However, the leader cannot abdicate the responsibility of clarifying his or her expectations for team members. Likewise, leaders should let team members know what to expect from them in the way of resources, advice, support, and counsel. Your job as a leader is to provide realistic expectations and acceptable standards of excellence. Leaders who strive for clarity in their expectations find that frustration is minimized and that team members experience greater work satisfaction and a deep sense of accomplishment.

Keeping Committed Team Members

Survey after survey concludes that the majority of the American work force would change jobs at the drop of a hat for equal money. The not-so-subtle message is that team members aren't overly concerned with compensation. What they want is an environment that offers the opportunity to grow in both skill and responsibility.

PAUL J. MEYER

This fundamental truth gives leaders another important responsibility: When delegating, leaders need to give team members the authority and resources required to complete the assignment. Leaders who hand out assignments without providing support undermine—if inadvertently—the credibility and motivation of their team members.

Highly effective leaders always seek ways to enhance the credibility of their team members. If someone is missing goals or making poor decisions, the best leaders choose to coach rather than criticize. Situations that impair productivity are actually opportunities in disguise—opportunities to teach a better way, to stimulate or improve critical thought, and to create even more effective procedures.

When you take advantage of negative situations by making them opportunities for growth, your team members develop and build their own competency. Their loyalty to you and their bond with the organization become stronger, and your authority is enhanced.

Burgeoning Entrepreneurship

Effective leaders are always on the lookout for ways to make use of the entrepreneurial tendencies among team members. Of course, the entrepreneurial spirit is critically important, but if every individual started his or her own business, there would be no one available to help run them!

Creative leaders understand that even a single organization can be structured so that any number of people are given almost complete responsibility and control over a particular segment of the business.

Giving team members ownership of their work attracts and keeps good people. Leaders who make the best use of team member creativity, initiative, and the quest for individual achievement are faced less often with replacing a member of the organization who has left for greener pastures.

Avoiding Leadership Pitfalls

Traps to Avoid

Busy leaders and managers with a strong achievement drive can sometimes fall into what might be called "leadership traps" that severely limit their potential success and even destroy individual creativity. Only when effective leaders are aware of these traps can they take the positive actions necessary to avoid them.

- *Doing Too Much:* The failure to delegate properly tends to trap unsuspecting leaders and managers under the pressure of too much paperwork, too many details to handle, and too little time for creative planning and management. Essentially, the leader's attitude is the culprit. Leaders who believe in their people, train them well, and give them the opportunity to accept responsibility for significant projects to avoid this problem altogether.

- *Doing Too Little:* Just as crippled and devastated as the leader who fails to delegate is the leader who over-delegates. Before giving authority and responsibility to team members, leaders must assure themselves that those individuals have been adequately trained, have "bought into" common goals, and are not already overburdened beyond their resources. Not doing enough results in an out-of-touch leader, someone who has lost control of the organization. Such a leader can no longer influence organizational direction. An effective leader avoids this pitfall by keeping an up-to-date, written plan for delegating, along with an implementation schedule and details of what is to be delegated...and to whom.

- *Failing to Recognize Personal Growth Needs:* In their concern for helping team members grow and improve, leaders may tend to neglect their own personal growth needs. Effective leaders never assume that they have learned all they need to learn, developed all the skills required for their continued success, or have become all that their potential allows. Any leader, regardless of status or stature, has even more potential for success available for immediate use. A plan of action for personal growth, coupled with decisive action toward goals in all six areas of life, will ensure adequate recognition of the leader's own need for personal growth.

- *Accepting Mediocre Performance*: All leaders learn that continual striving for excellence is, in and of itself, hard work. That's why many leaders and managers make the mistake of accepting mediocre performance from their team members and from themselves as well. What is "average" performance cannot be magically transformed into "good enough" for the leader or follower who aspires to real success and achievement. Highly effective leaders carry one standard—excellence. They demand outstanding results from themselves and all those who are associated with them. They continually monitor progress toward organizational goals, comparing current results to those obtained last month, last quarter, and last year. Then, they push for greater improvement.

- *Failing to Use Team Member Potential:* Many leaders find it easy enough to drift along, allowing their team members to do the same work they've always done. The problem with this approach is that doing what has always been done means getting what they've always gotten. It's a mistake to assume that past performance is a reliable indicator of how much your team members can really do. Effective leaders study their people; they learn team member strengths, desires, and personal goals. Leaders can then give team members the opportunity to develop new talents and abilities, and to make maximum use of skills already acquired. The best leaders offer team members the chance to acquire new ideas that will help each individual become more valuable to the organization and more personally fulfilled. When team members grow, the entire organization benefits.

- *Guarding the Status Quo:* When using and applying their valuable past experiences, many leaders rightly endeavor to stick to the basics—in other words, they cling to what works. This is good and well. As the saying goes, "If it ain't broke..." An important trap to avoid, however, is the subtle irrationality that forces a leader to maintain the status quo at the expense of losing the organization's cutting edge. Determining the right amount of change for you and your team is a delicate decision. On one end of the continuum is the status quo. At the other end is chaos. Highly effective leaders do not have the luxury of concentrating on only one end of this change continuum. Instead, they must attend to both ends—preserving the core *and* pioneering new territory. As you push the team and yourself to change and grow, yet keep your focus on the unique vision and mission of your company's past and future, your leadership bridge will lead to exciting and profitable territory. Work hard to preserve your organization's core; yet at the same time, pursue ambitious goals for growth and change. As you exercise your personal courage to initiate, inspire, and push for changes that will make your team even more competitive, and effectively communicate to your team members why these changes are worthwhile, they will begin to grow and change with you. They will emanate your excitement and enthusiasm for the work. And they have the security of knowing that you are not implementing change for the sake of change itself but for furthering the core mission and ideals of your company.

- *Ignoring Problems and Postponing Solutions:* Effective leaders recognize that there is but one best time to solve problems—before they occur! The most successful organizational goals programs anticipate potential roadblocks and incorporate plans for overcoming barriers if they do occur. Clear procedures, carefully designed, serve to prevent problems or provide for their proper handling. Crises are thus reduced to something akin to routine events. When problems occur, the best leaders handle them quickly. Complex problems may require extensive research and/or planning in order to reach the correct solution. But once a solution has been found, it should be implemented as quickly as possible. The temptation to wait until the problem has solved itself is nothing short of a deadly trap. This is because of the method in which problems solve themselves. Quite often, leaders and managers who procrastinate when problem solving discover that the problem is destroying the entire organization. This is an incredible waste. The problem might have been quickly solved using the combined creativity of team members and leaders alike.

- *Incomplete Communication:* It stands to reason that leaders and managers who encounter difficulty in effective delegation also may have trouble giving team members all the information they need. Other leaders may delegate but make the mistake of assuming that their employees already know everything necessary to complete the assigned task. And incomplete communication often results when leaders and managers fail to listen and creatively interpret the information and feedback offered by others. The best leaders are sound communicators who monitor the communication pulse or climate within their organization. Incomplete communication may be the most visible symbol of the leadership gap. Until effective leaders close the gap by empowering team members and helping them grow and improve, antiquated leadership and management styles will never really change.

The Challenge as Its Own Reward

The Benefits of Bridging the Leadership Gap

Developing your full potential as an effective leader involves an incredible amount of hard work. This is as it should be. Any kind of personal growth always requires effort, and developing your leadership skill is no exception. You may find that you achieve some leadership goals fairly quickly, with only a small investment of time, effort, and money. More significant leadership goals, however, may take a number of years to complete and may require nearly endless amounts of time and hard work on your part. But everything worth having—including the status of highly effective leadership—carries a unique price tag. Just as every worthwhile goal produces significant rewards, so your leadership success is equally rich in benefit for yourself and others.

The most evident returns on your investment in effective leadership are your position and financial rewards. These tangible benefits enable you to fulfill more basic needs and give you the freedom to devote time and attention to higher levels of needs and personal growth.

Additionally, leadership success earns you the respect and trust of your team members...and others outside the organization as well. As they follow you, your team members encourage you to become even more competent and more successful. You will find that their respect and trust for you are shared by other members of the community. In this way, you begin to exert a leadership influence that reaches far beyond the scope of the organization. Additionally, you find new and exciting opportunities for personal growth and service to others.

Your own awareness of your professional competence is a prime reward of your growth as an effective leader. For someone who is self-motivated and goal-directed, that sense of personal competence is a far more satisfying reward than the more tangible rewards that others seem to crave.

Your leadership competence shows that you possess a lofty and noble desire—the desire to attain some measure of lasting achievement and to contribute something valuable to the lives of other people.

Developing your leadership expertise enables you to reach significant personal goals. Professional success provides you with an income adequate for the necessities of life and for luxuries as well. You enjoy the freedom to structure and manage your own activities, and you garner the ability to move in and among social circles and professional organizations that interest you. Goals in other areas of life become more attainable as you continue to grow professionally and personally.

The Most Exciting Reward

At the core of leadership success lies the most exciting reward of all: the ability to offer new opportunities to other people. Your team members become like family members to you; you feel the same intense desire to help them grow and achieve their own personal goals. You find joy in helping your team members achieve their own personal goals and find satisfaction in their successes. You share their excitement as you reward their achievement with money, position, and other recognition. Knowing that you have made a direct contribution to the growth of the individuals on your team creates a unique sense of fulfillment—a fulfillment that probably cannot be found in any other way.

Your leadership success also enables you to serve your community at large. As an effective leader, you have the skills to contribute to the management and success of the various groups to which you belong...civic organizations, professional groups, religious and charitable organizations, and so on. Successful leadership is a magnet—it makes people seek you out and ask for your help. In this way, more than any other, you can expand your influence and heighten your impact on other people. This "being of service" benefit adds rich meaning and purpose to your life.

The Art of Giving

It probably goes without saying that leadership and management growth carry abundant financial rewards. How will you use them? Will you see yourself as their rightful owner with no further thought than your own interests? Or will you see yourself as a temporary steward of these assets, charged with empowering them to do the most good?

Encourage yourself and your colleagues to use the financial rewards of leadership to develop an enjoyment of giving. While we live in a world of abundance, it is an unfortunate fact that not everyone is able to enjoy the abundance. See your financial success as a vehicle that makes possible a college education for a deserving youngster, a badly needed operation for someone plagued by a health problem, or the solution to a housing problem that has burdened your community for decades.

PAUL J. MEYER

If helping your team members grow and improve helps you know great joy, you will also enjoy the immense satisfaction that comes from widening your circle of influence. Extend your efforts as far as possible...strive to give something back to your own community, your society, your nation, and the entire world. You will not regret the experience!

John F. Kennedy once said, "One person can make a difference, and everyone should try." The fact that comparatively few individuals really make a difference in this world attests to the rarity of true givers among us. Takers are abundant. Being a giver is truly a mark of high calling...and a natural for any effective leader striving to bridge the leadership gap.

A Postscript

The Choices We Face

Every leader has options and choices. Effective leaders possess the responsibility of deciding which options they want to pursue. While many people react with utter confusion when confronted by the challenges and choices of life, great achievers and leaders respond with confidence and certainty.

But many leaders often seem hesitant to make decisions. They seem to genuinely fear commitment to one course of action or another. Unfortunately for these individuals, the path across the leadership bridge requires a step-by-step decision-making process involving clear choices, clear objectives, and a concise plan of action to define the process of achieving those goals.

You may find that you are tempted to try to navigate the choppy seas of indecision by deciding not to decide...anything. Of course, your decision not to decide may not be a conscious thought. Instead, you may discover that you tend to make the determination subconsciously. For indecisive leaders, the end result is rather depressing: They achieve little in their lives and for their organizations, especially compared to their vast, untapped potential for achievement. Their failure to accomplish worthy goals can be blamed on their failure to decide *what* to accomplish.

For leaders and followers alike, a simple solution to this dilemma exists: All of us must, at some point, decide to decide. No one can offer only a half-hearted commitment to any of life's choices and challenges if they expect to master it and emerge a truly better person. Effective leaders strive to determine their objectives and focus on them with the zeal of a crusader. They understand that only complete and total commitment to achieving a goal ensures a successful undertaking.

Another Sort of Safety Net

The objectives you choose, however, can be altered slightly or changed completely. As a leader, you know that few plans of action are irreversible. If you or someone you lead determines at some point in the future that an incorrect choice has been made, the objective can be abandoned, and the process of decision making can begin all over again.

But be careful—because this safety net is not always a viable one. Neither leaders nor followers can continue trying option after option, discarding each one and eventually running out of time, energy, or money. The reversal of a decision cannot change faulty choices forever...sooner or later, reality intrudes, and the costs and consequences of those choices become inescapable.

If you and your team members have carefully evaluated where you stand now and determined where you want to go, you'll probably have specific goals already in mind. You may find that some answers temporarily conflict with each other.

Here, the challenge of choices comes full circle: You and your team members must decide which of your previous decisions means more to you than the other decisions you've made.

Highly effective leaders know that simply deciding on a goal doesn't make the goal a reality...or even achievable. Indeed, the decision-making process is only the first step. The first pillar of the Leadership Bridge requires crystallized thinking; the second demands a written plan to achieve the objective, with a deadline for its attainment. These piers must be solidly built before you and your team members can construct the rest of the leadership bridge.

Requirement for Achievement

No one can be truly successful without crystallized thinking and a concise plan for achievement. Such a plan will help you and your followers step-by-step through the process of developing and pursuing worthwhile goals. A time-tested tool is the Personal Plan of Action contained in all Paul J. Meyer programs. Using this Plan of Action is the simplest, most effective way to identify, clarify, and plan for the achievement of Total Person goals and objectives.

Why? Because a Paul J. Meyer program incorporates the best in personal development thinking...and it offers proven application as well. While the program makes you think, it also guides you step-by-step through the Total Person process. The program's Plan of Action offers the tools necessary to build the Leadership Bridge. No pillar of the bridge relies on guesswork—each tool has been designed for ease of use and maximum results.

The Plan of Action builds on the six areas of life. It gives you and your followers the opportunity to create a random list of things you'd like to see happen in each area of life. Self-evaluation questionnaires offer you and your team members concise insight into present status in each area of life.

Your Plan of Action moves through the development of values and priorities and offers point-by-point coaching through the thinking process required to plan for the achievement of important goals. By backing that plan with affirmations and visualization—two important tools for greater success and achievement—our clients develop the vehicle that will guide them to the success they desire.

No magic rays exist in a Paul J. Meyer program. Sitting on a bookshelf, the program cannot imbue anyone with success. Each program requires personal involvement...and that involvement continues as you think through the process, put forth the mental effort, and accept the challenges of success.

In the final analysis, a Paul J. Meyer program is the easiest, most effective route for any leader wishing to bridge the leadership gap.

The Next Step

To obtain more information about Paul J. Meyer programs in the United States, call Leadership Management Inc. at 1-800-568-1241. We'll introduce you to an LMI franchisee, dealer, or area director who will work with you to understand your unique situation. This individual will then be able to suggest a Paul J. Meyer program that will help you and your team members achieve the objectives you seek.

In other nations around the globe, call our international companies, headquartered in Waco, Texas, at 254-776-7551. We'll make sure that you get more information on international programs and courses.

Becoming Whole Again

Our company's concept teaches leaders and team members alike to become whole again. The bridge across the leadership gap is more than just an ideal; the concept of effective leadership is more than a simple catch phrase. Helping people become whole again is the essence of what we do. When leaders are not whole personally, they usually fail miserably in their efforts to direct the actions of others. Often, their own lives are destroyed in the process.

The end result we seek, of course, is the sharing of the Total Person concept with those who make your effort work. If you do not personally use the concept yourself, you cannot effectively share it. Trying to make others into something you are not is tantamount to going back to somewhere you have never been.

If you are trying to lead without becoming a Total Person and a highly effective leader, you cannot be certain of your destination...or even of the route you'll take. Enlisting the company of others on such an unplanned journey is perilous indeed. For your own sake—and for the sake of those you lead—strive to become what you were intended to be in each area of life.

When you've mastered the process yourself, you can share it with those who follow you. Working individually with your followers, you will begin to build a committed team. When members of the committed team begin to work together in the same way, a committed organization is created. The end result is that you will have changed the world—you will have done something to put people and society together for the benefit of all.

In all the annals of human history, few leaders have ever made a greater contribution.

Appendix 1

Questions at the Crossroads

These questions represent the crucible of highly effective leadership. They are also indicators of your progress in your personal efforts to build a leadership bridge. Can you answer all eleven questions with a resounding "Yes"?

Question One: Have I crystallized my thinking so that I know where I stand now and where I want to go?

Question Two: Are my vision, mission, and purpose clear to me and my team members?

Question Three: Do I have a detailed, written plan to achieve each important personal and organizational goal, and have I set a deadline for attainment?

Question Four: Are my personal goals balanced with the need to help my organization achieve?

Question Five: Do my personal goals represent a balance among the six areas of life?

Question Six: Do I have a burning desire to achieve the goals I have set for myself?

Question Seven: Have I developed within my team members and myself a passion for achieving the success we've envisioned?

Question Eight: Do I have supreme confidence in our ability to reach our goal?

Question Nine: Do I trust my team members to strive toward success and to continue to develop more of their innate potential for achievement?

Question Ten: Have I accepted personal responsibility for the success of my team—and for the achievement of my own personal goals?

Question Eleven: Do I possess the iron-willed determination to follow through regardless of circumstances or what others say, think, or do?

Appendix 2

Goals for the Six Areas of Life

The key to becoming a Total Person is to set and achieve meaningful goals in all six areas of life. In Chapter Five, we offered some suggested goals for each area.

In the spaces below, you can jot down ideas for goals in each area…goals that are personally meaningful to you and will motivate you to develop and use more of your full potential.

Goals for the Family Area:

Goals for the Financial Area:

Goals for the Mental Area:

Goals for the Physical Area:

Goals for the Social Area:

Goals for the Spiritual Area:

Appendix 3

The Question of Risk

I have lived a lifetime of thinking, planning, and then jumping in—taking a chance—and it has paid off handsomely for me.

People ask about different businesses I have started and how I knew when I had enough information to make an investment in real estate or any other venture. I tell them I always ask myself these questions:

What are my goals?

Can I reach my goal without taking a risk?

What are the benefits to gain if I take this chance?

What can I lose by taking a chance—by risking?

What can I do to prevent these losses?

Is the potential loss I am thinking about greater than the possible gain?

Is this the right time to take this action?

What pressures are on me to make this decision?

What would I have to know to change my mind about taking this risk?

What experience do I have taking this type of risk?

Who is someone I can confide in or ask for advice about this risk?

Do I have personal blind spots in my vision about this risk?

If I take this chance, this risk, will people think more of me or less of me if I succeed? Do I really care?

If a loss does occur, will I take it personally, or am I able to be realistic and objective about it?

Will I worry about the risk I have taken?

Who else has made a similar investment?

What actions can I take to track my investment and protect it?

How will this risk affect me, my family, my friends, my company, and my relationship with my bank?

Do I really enjoy the lifestyle of an entrepreneur?

Fortunately, anything that has ever happened to me in my role as a salesperson, a businessperson, an investor, has never affected who I am as a person or reduced my self-image. I make a conscious decision to manage my life to maintain a healthy self-image, peace of mind, and happiness.

PAUL J. MEYER

A Final Word

In My Father's Hand

Years ago, my father copied a Will Allen Dromgoole poem onto a page of a ruled tablet. I kept the poem for years, folded and tucked into my wallet. Today, it hangs in my office, a reminder of the attitudes and values my parents worked to instill in my brother, my sister, and me.

> *An old man traveling a lone highway,*
> *Came at evening, cold and gray,*
> *To a chasm deep and wide;*
> *The old man crossed in the twilight dim,*
> *The sullen stream held no fear for him,*
> *But he turned when he reached the other side,*
> *And builded a bridge to span the tide.*
> *Old man, cried a fellow pilgrim near,*
> *You are wasting your strength with your building here.*
> *You never again will pass this way,*
> *Your journey will end with the ending day.*
> *You have crossed the chasm deep and wide,*

Why build this bridge at eventide?
But the builder raised his old gray head,
Good friend, in the path I have come, he said,
There followeth after me today,
A youth whose feet must pass this way,
This chasm which has been naught to me,
To that fair-headed youth may a pitfall be;
He, too, must cross in the twilight dim,
Good friend, I am building this bridge for him.

Carl August Meyer was a German immigrant. His legacy to his three children—and through us, to the world—has been the foundation for my efforts to help individuals and organizations across the globe build their bridge to span the leadership gap.

PAUL J. MEYER